D1145274

The GAO

UNTAPPED SOURCE

OF CONGRESSIONAL POWER

The
GAO

UNTAPPED SOURCE

OF CONGRESSIONAL POWER

By Richard E. Brown

WITH A FOREWORD BY

SENATOR WILLIAM PROXMIRE

THE UNIVERSITY OF TENNESSEE PRESS
KNOXVILLE

LIBRARY OF CONGRESS CATALOG CARD NO. 78–111049
STANDARD BOOK NO. 87049–120–2

Copyright © 1970 by The University of Tennessee Press.
Manufactured in the United States of America.
All Rights Reserved. First Edition.

FOREWORD

FEW people have heard of the General Accounting Office. Few know what it does. Fewer still know that it is an arm of the United States Congress. This book tells a great deal about this indispensable organization.

Not only is the GAO called the "watchdog" of the government, but it deserves that reputation. For every one dollar spent for its operations, it saves at least three dollars through its reports, audits, and actions. Indirectly, it saves many times that much. In my view its direct and indirect savings amount to many billions a year.

This book began as a case study of the GAO and its relationship to the Tennessee Valley Authority. Professor Brown has extended that original plan so that the book encompasses far more than its original objective. That is all to the good, for the GAO has changed significantly in its scope and activities in recent years.

For my own part I find its activities vital to the proper functioning of the Congress. Without it and its powers to audit and investigate, the Congress would be almost powerless in its watchdog and oversight functions. In addition, the GAO is almost the only institution on which Congress can rely to offset the one-sided and ex-parte requests of the executive agencies for funds.

Since the early New Deal days, political scientists and political commentators have tended to glorify and even to canonize the executive branch of the government. It could do no wrong. Meanwhile, Congress was personified largely as a bunch of country bumpkins whose interests in local projects or fence-mending made it a useless appendage in the modern world.

Reality is a very different matter. Almost every major piece of reform legislation has been initiated by some member of Congress, not by the executive. The bureaucracy by nature plays it safe, plumps for the *status quo*, and attempts to build up its own political empire. There is little place for the free spirit who questions or criticizes programs or events. The Air Force fired A. E. Fitzgerald when he correctly testified that there was a $2 billion overrun on the C5A. Rather than reform its practices, the Air Force got rid of its critic.

Congress has rightly resisted the setting up of its own operating counterpart to the administrative agencies. It has correctly, in my view, kept its staff small and its operating functions limited. But this is only possible because of the oversight and watchdog functions of the GAO. In my view, those functions should not be limited. They should be expanded.

The world thinks of accountants as thin, middle-aged, balding milquetoasts who pore over deadly dull figures while wearing a green eyeshade. That was never the reality of the GAO. It has always been an active, forthright, honest, and prestigious organization which has served individual congressmen and senators as well as congressional committees. This reality should not be changed. As an individual senator I receive at least one letter a week charging waste, corruption, or wrong-doing which I send on to the GAO to investigate and confirm.

It was just such a letter from John McGee in Thailand, charging graft and corruption in the distribution of American gasoline, oil, and jet fuel, which led to the GAO investigation that confirmed his charges. Typically, the administrative agency involved, in this case the Navy, whitewashed those responsible for the corruption and reprimanded John McGee. But without the GAO, McGee's charges could never have been proved. The Navy would have covered up entirely.

I would resist strongly any attempt to limit the services of the GAO merely to the committees of the Congress. The individual House or Senate member must have access to them. The tendency to act as though the committees were the Congress, rather than the creatures of the House or Senate and subordinate to them, is a practice which has gone too far.

But even though it has carried out its functions well and acted with a sense of rugged independence befitting an agency whose head is insulated from popular pressure through a fifteen-year appointment, the GAO also has had to live in the real world. It too gets its funds from the House and Senate appropriations committees. It too is overseen by the government operations committees. The GAO is not unaware of these facts of life, and occasionally it is not as aggressive as it might otherwise be if such were not true.

A case in point was the long-standing failure of the GAO to make critical examinations of military weapons systems. Its failure in this area was no worse than that of the Bureau of the Budget, the military services, and the armed services and government operations committees of Congress itself. But the fact was that until my subcommittee exposed the huge overrun on the C5A, the General Accounting Office had largely contented itself in examining the sufficiency of the military supply systems and had avoided examining the weapons systems themselves.

Under various amendments to the military authorization bills this situation has now been remedied, and the GAO's function in this area is in the forefront of the fight to bring military spending under control.

All in all, Congress could not carry out its main function of controlling the purse strings without the General Accounting Office. In the hiring of economists, systems analysts, and experts in modern cost-effectiveness techniques, Comptroller General Elmer B. Staats is moving to make the GAO even better prepared to deal with modern budgeting and spending issues than it has been in the past. I welcome this broadening of the GAO horizons.

In describing the GAO and in shaping these issues, this book is an important contribution to public understanding of the Congress, the GAO, and their work.

WILLIAM PROXMIRE
UNITED STATES SENATE

ACKNOWLEDGMENTS

I am happy to acknowledge the many debts I incurred while carrying out my research preparation of this volume. Professors Samuel H. Beer, Arthur A. Maass, and Don K. Price, of Harvard University, and Roscoe C. Martin of Syracuse University, all read the manuscript at some stage and offered numerous helpful suggestions. I was fortunate to develop a working relationship with Professor Gordon S. Reid, newly appointed professor of politics at The Australian National University, Canberra, who was for a time visiting professor of government at The College of William and Mary on The National Science Foundation Distinguished Foreign Scientist Fellowship Program. Professor Reid made many valuable comments on the comparative government aspects of my manuscript, especially in relation to Australian and British government. Without the invaluable assistance of many officials of the U.S. General Accounting Office, this study could not have been completed. The names of most of these officials are shown in the bibliography, but a special mention should be made of a few: Owen A. Kane coordinated my research work in the GAO and arranged interviews for me with Comptroller General Elmer B. Staats, Assistant Comptroller General Robert F. Keller and former Assistant Comptroller General Frank H. Weitzel, among others. In addition, GAO officials E. H. Morse and Lawrence J. Powers made careful and important reviews of the manuscript to ensure technical accuracy. I must also mention the valuable assistance of many congressional staff members and TVA officials—most of whose names are also shown in the bibliography.

In recognizing the assistance of others, I am certain every

reader will appreciate that the views expressed and conclusions drawn are my responsibility alone. Indeed, I should establish now that a few of those who assisted me most in my research and writing do not agree with some of my interpretations and conclusions. It is also important now to say a word about references in the text to information received from individuals. Because all the persons interviewed were employees of the government, and because some asked that information not be attributed to them, footnote references to specific persons are not made, and direct quotes from interview sources are not generally used in the text.

There remains a special kind of debt to acknowledge—the one to my wife and children. To them I offer my deepest thanks and appreciation for their help and patience, and to them I dedicate this work.

RICHARD E. BROWN

Williamsburg, Virginia
June, 1970

CONTENTS

The GAO

UNTAPPED SOURCE

OF CONGRESSIONAL POWER

I. INTRODUCTION

Scarcely a day goes by that the U.S. Congress is not taken to task on television or radio or in the newspapers for the way it has handled some important issue. Although most Americans do not dwell on the matter, they are likely to be vaguely suspicious that all is not well on Capitol Hill. Doubts and unkind feelings abound regarding the work and responsibilities of Congress; its methods of conducting business; and its strength, vigor, and effectiveness as compared to the executive branch of the government.

Indeed, a vast and growing literature is devoted to analyzing and commenting on congressional operations, ranging in recent years from the scholarly American Assembly's *The Congress and America's Future* to the highly practical *Management Study of the U.S. Congress,* by Arthur D. Little, Inc., consulting firm, prepared for the National Broadcasting Company's special television report "Congress Needs Help." An article in *The Reader's Digest,* "Is Congress Destroying Itself," attests to the more popular concern with congressional affairs.[1] The underlying question of these and similar studies may be stated generally as follows:

---

[1] David B. Truman, ed., *The Congress and America's Future* (Englewood Cliffs, N. J.: Prentice-Hall, Inc., 1965); Arthur D. Little, Inc., *Management Study of the U.S. Congress* (Cambridge, Mass., 1965); Eugene H. Methvin, "Is Congress Destroying Itself?," *The Reader's Digest* (Apr., 1969), pp. 65–70. See also, among others, Richard Bolling, *House Out of Order* (New York: E. P. Dutton and Co., Inc., 1965); Joseph S. Clark, *Congress: The Sapless Branch* (New York: Harper and Row, Publishers, 1964); Charles L. Clapp, *The Congressman: His Work As He Sees It* (Washington, D.C.: Brookings Institution, 1963); George B. Galloway, *Congress at the Crossroads* (New York: Thomas Y. Crowell Company, 1946); Philip Donham and Robert J. Fahey, *Congress Needs Help*

In an age when the executive bureaucracy is growing rapidly in size, stature, and competence, when problems continue to increase in complexity, and when fast and decisive action is often imperative, how can Congress continue to perform its many duties wisely and well?

As implied by the question itself, the search for an answer is complicated by the intricacy of congressional duties. Among its other tasks, Congress must exercise effective supervision and control over the executive branch, function as an equal and imaginative partner in the governmental system, ensure that congressional laws are administered in accord with true congressional intent, make appropriations expeditiously and thoughtfully, and obtain the necessary information for wise lawmaking. The effective performance of these duties would be formidable enough for congressmen even if they were not forced, at the same time, to devote considerable energy just to the problem of remaining in office. Thus, as most analyses have concluded, Congress does need help.

Although the need is generally acknowledged, there has been no widespread agreement among political scientists on the problem of meeting it. Toward a solution of this problem, this brief volume makes no far-reaching proposals to alter our existing governmental system. Instead, it merely suggests the fuller use by Congress of an existing tool—the U.S. General Accounting Office (GAO)—which is showing an increasing capacity to serve Congress. Its potential for further and better aid, moreover, appears to be almost unlimited.

While American scholars in recent years have directed their attention with deeper insight and renewed vigor to the study of the politics of the nation's legislatures,[2] they have given surpris-

---

(New York: Random House, 1966); and Alfred de Grazia, ed., *Congress: The First Branch of Government* (Garden City, N. Y.: Anchor Books, Doubleday and Company, Inc., 1967).

[2] See, for example, in addition to some of those listed in the previous note, the following works: Richard F. Fenno, Jr., *The Power of the Purse: Appropriations Politics in Congress* (Boston: Little, Brown and Company, 1966); Harold P. Green and Alan Rosenthal, *Government of*

ingly little attention to the GAO. The scope and usefulness of the GAO are described, if at all, only in general terms. In particular, little is known today about important changes made since World War II in the direction and emphasis of the agency's work. Many students of government continue to think of the GAO as it was delineated in Harvey Mansfield's *The Comptroller General,* an excellent work, but as of the year 1939.[3] Accordingly, critics are prone to make charges against the GAO that are based largely on a lack of complete, current information—or else the charges reflect a bias toward the executive branch of the government and the theory of strong executive power. As a result, the work and potential of the GAO have been largely obscured from the view of educators and the American public alike.

The GAO is a unique governmental agency charged with assisting Congress in supervising the operations of the executive branch of the government. Its scope and duties, as defined by law and congressional directives, are to be found in a 1962 Senate document in which the GAO is called "a nonpolitical nonpartisan agency in the legislative branch of the Government created by the Congress to act in its behalf in examining the manner in which Government agencies discharge their financial responsibilities with regard to public funds appropriated or otherwise made available to them by the Congress and to make recom-

---

the Atom (New York: Atherton Press, 1964); Robert L. Peabody and Nelson W. Polsby, *New Perspectives on the House of Representatives* (Chicago: Rand McNally and Co., 1963); William J. Keefe and Morris S. Ogul, *The American Legislative Process: Congress and the States* (Englewood Cliffs, N. J.: Prentice-Hall, Inc., 1964); Kenneth Kofmehl, *Professional Staffs of Congress* (Lafayette, Indiana: Purdue University Studies, 1962); John S. Saloma, III, *The Responsible Use of Power: A Critical Analysis of the Congressional Budget Process* (Washington, D.C.: American Enterprise Institute for Public Policy Research, 1964); and Ralph K. Huitt and Robert L. Peabody, *Congress: Two Decades of Analysis* (New York: Harper and Row, Publishers, 1969). The last work, by Huitt and Peabody, contains an excellent discussion on research on Congress, as well as an extensive and useful bibliography.

[3] Harvey C. Mansfield, *The Comptroller General: A Study in the Law and Practice of Financial Administration* (New Haven: Yale University Press, 1939).

mendations looking to greater economy and efficiency in public expenditures."[4]

To discharge this important duty, the GAO works in seven specific areas: (1) It audits the activities, financial transactions, and accounts of the federal government and reports the results thereof to Congress. (2) It prescribes accounting principles, standards, and related requirements; cooperates in the development and improvement of agency accounting and financial management systems; and reviews and approves agency accounting systems. (3) It settles claims by and against the federal government. (4) It collects debts for the government arising from adjudicated claims and amounts reported by government departments and agencies as uncollectible through means available to them. (5) It performs legal work, rendering decisions at the request of heads of departments and agencies, and disbursing and certifying officers on the legality of proposed payments or transactions—decisions that are binding on the executive branch. (6) It gives special assistance to Congress by making special audits, surveys, and investigations at the request of congressional committees and members of Congress, furnishing information in reply to inquiries, assigning personnel to assist congressional committees, and furnishing comments on proposed legislation. (7) It manages records, preserving and servicing disbursing officers' accounts, vouchers, certificates, and related papers until they are disposed of as provided by law.[5]

The focus of this examination of the GAO will be on the agency's auditing and related investigative activities, since these two functions give the GAO a special opportunity to make an invaluable contribution to Congress in carrying out its own enormous responsibilities. To explore in detail the GAO's total responsibilities could easily become confusing and further obscure the area

[4] U.S., Congress, Senate, Committee on Government Operations, *Functions of the General Accounting Office*, 87th Cong., 2d sess., 1962, Doc. No. 96, p. 1. This document and General Accounting Office, *Annual Reports of the Comptroller General of the United States* (Washington, D.C.: U.S. Government Printing Office, published annually) are two of the best sources of information on the work of the GAO.

[5] General Accounting Office, *Annual Report, 1968*, pp. 251–52.

of the GAO's greatest potential. Another self-imposed limitation of this volume is the choice of a single governmental agency—the Tennessee Valley Authority (TVA)—to serve as the analytical tool for depicting how, specifically, the GAO's audit work serves Congress and for describing in some detail the GAO's relations with those whose activities it audits.

The selection of one agency for this purpose permits a degree of concentration and thus allows us to view the government as it really operates, on a day-to-day basis. Few dramatic or sensational audit findings or issues are presented here, a fact that should not be surprising, for the intricacies of most government business, like those of any other business, only rarely provide exciting material for popular consumption. Most of the GAO's work with Congress and with the various departments, whether TVA or some other agency, would be considered commonplace by the headline seeker, although the GAO has been in the newspaper headlines on many occasions in recent years, as we shall see. Lack of sensationalism, however, in no way detracts from the obvious importance of the agency's work to the congressional control of the nation's business.

Moreover, in terms of dollars, the activities and programs of the Tennessee Valley Authority are sizable. TVA's actual expenditures for fiscal year 1968, for example, were close to $550 million, although over $450 million of this total was for the agency's power program. Equally important, TVA is "representative" in that its work covers many areas of governmental concern: water, power, agricultural, and forest development; urban, education, and health problems; recreation activities; and research and construction.[6]

Aside from these considerations, the choice of TVA in particular allows us to present both sides of the story of the landmark feuds and agreements that characterized the earlier relations between the two agencies. Virtually all writers who have dealt extensively with either the GAO or the TVA have touched on this

[6] Tennessee Valley Authority, *Budget Program for Fiscal Year 1970* (Knoxville, 1969), beginning summary statements.

story; hence, this volume might be considered a continuation of that tradition. Fortunately, too, for our purpose, research sources were readily available: the files of TVA's general manager and other TVA records and documents; GAO files, annual reports, and audit reports of TVA; and congressional committee reports, studies, and hearings. These sources have been supplemented by many face-to-face discussions with officials of both organizations and with congressional staff members.

Endorsing this method of using the particular to explain the general, political scientist James Fesler says, "Progress in the science of administration must build on the description and appraisal of particular bodies of administrative experience. Without the solid grounding of case studies, generalization becomes mere opinion. And without reliable generalization there can be no science."[7] More recently, Lucian Pye wrote: "We would observe that the 'mere' descriptive study that 'only' tells us how a particular institution or process actually operates has accomplished a great deal indeed at this or any conceivable state of the social sciences. To ask for more is to reveal a lack of interest in the dynamics of the real world."[8]

[7] James W. Fesler, *Area and Administration* (University, Ala.: University of Alabama Press, 1949), pp. 117–18.

[8] Lucian W. Pye, "Description, Analysis, and Sensitivity to Change," in Austin Ranney, ed., *Political Science and Public Policy* (Chicago: Markham Publishing Company, 1968), p. 247.

II. DEVELOPMENT OF
"THE CONGRESSIONAL WATCHDOG"

T HE U.S. General Accounting Office, created by the Budget and Accounting Act of 1921 as the national public auditing agency, is the result and embodiment of more than two hundred years of remarkably consistent thinking on the necessity of the public audit. In a representative form of government, legislative control of federal funds is considered basic; and although this control takes various administrative forms in representative governments throughout the world, in the United States the Constitution gives final authority over public finances to Congress by assigning to the House of Representatives exclusively the right to introduce tax bills and by giving Congress as a whole the power to lay and collect taxes, to borrow money on the credit of the United States, and to coin money.[1] By its very nature the public audit tests and ensures public accountability by obligating the GAO to present to Congress upon request all available information concerning the administration of federal funds. Thus, the audit serves as a preventive control, ferreting out illegality, fraud, waste, and extravagance and reporting on the soundness of policies, programs, and projects.

Accountability is the test without which control by elected and representative legislatures cannot be assured, without which the use of governmental power is left in doubt. Accountability is

[1] Harvey C. Mansfield and Fritz Morstein Marx, "Fiscal Accountability," in Marx, ed., *Elements of Public Administration* (Englewood Cliffs, N. J.: Prentice-Hall, Inc., 1959); and U.S., Congress, Senate, Committee on Government Operations, *Financial Management in the Federal Government,* 87th Cong., 1st sess., 1961, Doc. No. 11, Pt. 1.

venerable. As E. L. Normanton observes, it is an idea that "is perhaps as old as organized government. It was highly developed in classical Athens and was a matter of pride and principle."[2] And accountability is essential. As Normanton again tells us, it is "a constant reminder that government and administration are not activities intended solely for the benefit of those who practice them—a simple fact, but one which, Heaven knows, it is easy to forget."[3]

Until the Budget and Accounting Act created the GAO, Congress relied on two main devices for the surveillance and control of public fiscal activities: the language of the appropriation acts, and a set of internal checks within the executive branch. Appropriation acts were written in great detail in an effort to control and guide the use of the funds appropriated. The internal administrative checks were designed to ensure that, at each point in the expenditure of funds, a different official would have to verify the transaction, thus providing a measure of safety. These two devices were supplemented occasionally by congressional committee investigations.

However, the combination of these devices proved inadequate. Use of detailed appropriation language led, in time, to excessive specificity and proved self-defeating as executive departments struggled for a degree of administrative flexibility. Many devices were used, very often successfully, to circumvent congressional intent, including transfers of funds, the carrying forward of unexpended balances, and the incurring of obligations in anticipation of deficiency or future appropriations. The concept of internal administrative checks suffered a similar fate. Delays and confusion in the financial chain became commonplace, creating critical problems for the Treasury Department and its accounting system. These weaknesses in the apparatus of surveillance led to reform efforts beginning with the Dockery

[2] E. L. Normanton, *Accountability and Audit of Governments: A Comparative Study* (New York: Praeger Publishers, Inc., and Manchester University Press, Manchester, 1966), p. 3.

[3] *Ibid.*, p. 426.

Act of 1894 and culminating in the Budget and Accounting Act, which created the GAO.[4]

In the further interest of accountability, it was considered important to keep the two top officials of the GAO—the comptroller general and the assistant comptroller general—free of political involvement. Accordingly, they are appointed by the President subject to Senate confirmation, their terms run to fifteen years, and they are subject to removal only by joint resolution of Congress for specified causes or by impeachment. These conditions put the GAO beyond executive control. The agency has been declared to be "independent of the executive departments" and "a part of the legislative branch of the government."[5]

The present influence and authority of the GAO are the result of a gradual development. The Budget and Accounting Act of 1921 not only transferred audit responsibilities from the Treasury Department in the executive branch to the GAO in the legislative branch but also broadened the scope of audit work by requiring the comptroller general to investigate all matters relating to the receipt, disbursement, and application of public funds and to recommend measures that might lead to greater economy in public expenditure. And still further, the act directed the GAO to make whatever investigations and reports might be needed by either the House or the Senate or by any congressional committee having jurisdiction over revenue, appropriations, or expenditures.

Until 1945 only a few government corporations were audited by the GAO. But the Government Corporation Control Act of that year made all such corporations subject to the GAO and established these conditions: that the financial transactions of the government corporations were to be audited according to the same principles and procedures that applied to commercial corpora-

---

[4] Mansfield and Marx, "Fiscal Accountability," pp. 550–55.

[5] U.S., *42 Statutes at Large* 20 (1921) and *59 Statutes at Large* 616 (1945). An organization chart of the GAO is included here as app. A; a list of comptrollers general and assistant comptrollers general is included as app. B.

tions; that the audits were to be conducted at the place where the corporation's accounts were normally kept; and that reports of the audits were to be made to Congress not later than January 15 following the close of the fiscal year for which the audit was made.

The Legislative Reorganization Act of 1946 gave the House Committee on Expenditures and the Senate Committee on Expenditures (later, in 1952, these committees were renamed, respectively, the House [Senate] Committee on Government Operations) a definite place in the scheme of financial control exercised by the GAO. Until this act was passed, Congress was conspicuously indifferent to the work of the GAO. But the new act stipulated that these House and Senate committees would receive and examine reports of the GAO. Section 206 of the act directed the comptroller general to make an expenditure analysis of each agency in the executive branch to help Congress determine whether public funds had been used economically and efficiently.

It is this section 206 of the 1946 act that many American political scientists have viewed as an opportunity both to improve the congressional role in the budgetary process and to enhance the value of the GAO as a congressional aid. It is understandable, therefore, that these scholars are critical of Congress for its failure either to clarify the meaning of section 206 or to appropriate funds which the GAO may use to carry out section 206.[6]

In 1950, with passage of the Budget and Accounting Procedures Act, the comptroller general, the secretary of the treasury, and the director of the Bureau of the Budget were authorized to conduct a continuous program for the improvement of accounting and financial reporting, commonly referred to as the joint accounting improvement program. In carrying out this program the comptroller general had four specific duties: to prescribe the principles, standards, and related requirements for

[6] For example, see Robert A. Wallace, *Congressional Control of Federal Spending* (Detroit: Wayne State University Press, 1960), especially chs. 11 and 12, by permission of Wayne State University Press; and Saloma, *The Responsible Use of Power,* pp. 38–39, 81. Sec. 206 of the 1946 act will be discussed in more detail later in this book.

each executive agency; to cooperate with these agencies in the development of their accounting systems; to review these systems periodically and report to Congress; and to audit the financial transactions of each executive, legislative, and judicial agency. In addition, the 1950 act permits and encourages on-site audits of a comprehensive nature; that is, a study of the administrative practices of the agencies as well as a review of their financial transactions.

The 1950 act, in effect, elevated to formal legal status two programs that were begun earlier on an informal basis by the GAO: the joint accounting improvement program and the comprehensive audit program. The latter program grew out of the GAO's experience in carrying out the commercial-type audit required by the 1945 Government Corporation Control Act.[7]

Up to this point the status of the GAO could be assumed to be one of unimpeded progress. But the agency has had its share of adverse criticism and difficult times. As far back as 1937, the President's Committee on Administrative Management, consisting of Louis Brownlow (chairman), Luther Gulick, and Charles E. Merriam, reported that "for the purpose of providing the Chief Executive with the essential vehicles for current financial management and administrative control, the authority to prescribe and supervise accounting systems, forms and procedures . . . should be transferred to and vested in the Secretary of the Treasury." In the GAO's favor, however, this committee also recommended that the executive branch be made more truly

---

[7] This description of the major legislation affecting the development and work of the GAO is taken chiefly from the following accounts: General Accounting Office, *Annual Report, 1961*, pp. 5–7; and U.S., Congress, House, Committee on Government Operations, *The General Accounting Office: A Study of Its Organization and Administration with Recommendations for Increasing Effectiveness*, 84th Cong., 2d sess., 1956, Rept. 2264, pp. 13–15. App. A to this House committee report contains the most relevant parts of these acts. This document, along with the two pieces cited below, also offers some interesting information on the origins of the GAO: U.S., Congress, House, Committee on Expenditures in the Executive Departments, *The General Accounting Office: A Study of Its Functions and Operations*, 81st Cong., 1st sess., 1949, Rept. 1441; and Mansfield, *The Comptroller General*, cited previously.

accountable to Congress by a more searching and constructive post-audit by the GAO.[8]

The President's committee was merely underlining the commonly espoused opinion of many GAO critics: that the location of both the accounting and the auditing functions in a single congressional agency was anathema to all principles of good public administration. Of this attitude, Charles Hyneman states that "the position taken by the President's Committee seems to have been accepted as gospel by the academic students of government, hardly a murmur of dissent from its recommendations having appeared in the literature from 1937 until the appearance of the report of the Hoover Commission in 1949."[9]

The Hoover Commission on Organization of the Executive Branch of the Government, referred to by Hyneman, split internally on the issue of lodging both accounting and auditing functions in a single agency before making its final recommendations, which were very close to those of the President's committee of 1937. The Hoover Commission commended the progress of the comptroller general, the secretary of the treasury, and the director of the budget for having worked since 1947 to establish a joint accounting improvement program to encourage individual agencies to upgrade their own accounting practices. But, the Commission continued, "more than voluntary correctives are needed. A definite system should be established and given permanence through legislation and organization . . . . Since accounting is primarily the responsibility of the executive branch, it is proposed that this official should be an Accountant General in charge of a new Accounting Service in the Treasury Department." Rarely noted, however, is that in addition to disagreement among Commission members on the issue of combining accounting and auditing functions in the GAO, both the secretary of the treasury and the director of the Bureau of the

---

[8] U.S., The President's Committee on Administrative Management, *Report of the Committee, with Studies of Administrative Management in the Federal Government* (Washington, D.C.: U.S. Government Printing Office, 1937), pp. 24–25.

[9] Charles S. Hyneman, *Bureaucracy in a Democracy* (New York: Harper and Brothers, Publishers, 1950), p. 368.

Budget advised against accepting the Hoover Commission recommendation in the belief that the cooperative efforts of the three agencies provided an arrangement for solving government-wide accounting problems.[10]

The Commission criticized the GAO for its requirement that all expenditure vouchers and other data for every transaction of the noncorporate agencies be sent to its Washington office. To correct this situation, it recommended that the GAO perform its auditing work on a sampling basis at the place where an agency's records were kept. The GAO took immediate steps to follow these recommendations. It was this first Hoover Commission report that led to the Budget and Accounting Procedures Act of 1950. Thus, with the passage of the 1950 act, the work of the joint accounting improvement program was essentially written into law, and thenceforth the GAO followed the Hoover Commission's recommendations for on-site, spot-sampling procedures and more comprehensive audits.[11]

A second Hoover Commission in 1955 was again highly complimentary of the joint accounting improvement program. But it urged several further improvements in agency accounting and reporting: that the work be under the leadership of the Bureau of the Budget; that all agencies create the position of comptroller to manage their accounting activities; and that several more technical improvements be instituted, such as an allotment system for preventing appropriation deficiencies, accrual and cost accounting, property accounting, and disbursement accounting.[12]

As if in summary, John Millett wrote that "by 1955 many of

[10] U.S., Congress, Senate, Committee on Government Operations, *Financial Management*, pp. 65–67.

[11] U.S., Commission on Organization of the Executive Branch of the Government, *The Hoover Commission Report* (New York, McGraw-Hill Book Company, Inc., 1949), pp. 49–55, and, for the 1950 act, U.S., Congress, House, Committee on Government Operations, *The General Accounting Office*, pp. 70–78. See also General Accounting Office, *15 Years of Progress—Improvement of Financial Management in the U.S. Government* (Washington, D.C.: U.S. Government Printing Office, 1963); and *Joint Financial Management Improvement Program, 20th Annual Report, 1948–1968* (Washington, D.C.: U.S. Government Printing Office, 1968).

[12] U.S., Commission on Organization of the Executive Branch of the

the objections to the work of the General Accounting Office voiced by the President's Committee on Administrative Management in 1937 had been met . . . the Congress of the United States had acquired a powerful instrument for keeping the financial operations of government under continuing surveillance."[13] There is no doubt that the comptroller general continues to settle accounts for unincorporated as well as corporate agencies. But this control now involves more of a post-audit than it had earlier. And while the comptroller general retained his power to suspend or disallow items in the accounts of disbursing and certifying officers in noncorporate agencies, this power has also been used increasingly as a post-audit device to check on the legality and accuracy of transactions and not as a means of substituting his judgment for that of the administrative officials in advance.[14]

I

The GAO has now been compressed into a relatively small organization, from about 15,000 employees at the end of World War II and 5,400 in 1958 to approximately 4,500 in 1969. Just as significant as this great decrease, however, is the change in the composition of the work force. During the decade 1959–69, for example, while the GAO's total staff was reduced by 660 employees or over 12 percent, the number of professional auditors and accountants was increased substantially. Indeed, the present GAO staff of 4,500 includes over 2,600 accountants and auditors and 100 attorneys. This personnel shift reflects the GAO's increasing emphasis on professional audits and evaluations of governmental programs as opposed to the mere checking of financial details. GAO's "new look," including its increased use of the comprehensive-audit approach, has increased the agency's usefulness

---

Government, *Digests and Analyses of the Nineteen Hoover Commission Reports* (Washington, D.C.: Citizens Committee for the Hoover Report, 1955), pp. 177–90.

[13] John D. Millett, *Government and Public Administration: The Quest for Responsible Performance* (New York: McGraw-Hill Book Company, Inc., 1959), pp. 188–89.

[14] These points are developed more fully in later chapters.

to Congress and, thereby, has enhanced its prestige in the eyes of congressmen.[15]

In 1969 about 2,600 employees worked in the GAO headquarters building near Capitol Hill in Washington, D.C., another 1,800 were in regional offices in 42 principal cities on the United States mainland, and over 100 were stationed in Frankfurt, Honolulu (still considered a foreign office by the GAO), Manila, New Delhi, and Saigon to make audits of U.S. operations abroad. The Saigon office, the most recently acquired, was established in part to fulfill a request of the Foreign Operations and Government Information Subcommittee of the House Government Operations Committee.

The fiscal year 1969 appropriation for GAO activities was $59.6 million. For this same period refunds and collections made by or through the efforts of the GAO amounted to $20.4 million. The GAO also took credit for $167.2 million representing additional savings or increased revenues made possible by improved practices in government departments. Of this latter amount, approximately $65.0 million was recurring in nature and would therefore continue in future years.[16]

The GAO has come to serve Congress directly in a variety of ways. Its representatives testify before congressional committees, and it assigns staff members for temporary work with congressional committees, issues reports on pending bills to committee chairmen, and submits various periodic and special audit reports on government activities. In addition to the more formal audit reports, the agency makes other reviews and investigations of government operations, some of which are ultimately issued as audit reports.

Audit reports, because they afford written records that can easily be analyzed, will receive particular attention in the following chapters. There is certainly no dearth of this material, for in 1969 the GAO issued 1,023 audit reports, distributed as fol-

[15] General Accounting Office, *Annual Report, 1969*, p. 7; employment data sheet from GAO files; also interviews with GAO officials and congressional committee staff members.

[16] General Accounting Office, *Annual Report, 1969*, pp. 6–7, 380, 386; interviews with GAO officials.

lows: 177 reports went to Congress (these reports were initiated by GAO in areas of congressional interest and major dollar impact; GAO reports to Congress are public reports); 204 reports went to congressional committees and individual members in response to specific requests (during the past three fiscal years, GAO effort in this area has increased nearly 100 percent); and 642 reports, usually in the form of letters, went to officials of U.S. departments and agencies (these reports dealt largely with financial management systems and management practices). Breaking the total down another way, 519 reports pertained to the activities of the civil departments and agencies and also to the legislative branch, 438 to activities of the Department of Defense, 57 to international activities (including military and economic assistance to foreign countries), 6 to government-wide activities, and 3 to organizations outside government.[17]

II

As noted earlier, one of the most dramatic confrontations of the GAO has been with the TVA. Critics often use the differences between these two agencies as an example of the GAO's ineffectiveness in its early years. For example, Harvey Mansfield, in *The Comptroller General,* considers the controversy significant in the development of both the GAO and the TVA and discusses it at some length. Only the highlights of the controversy can be given here, but they are basic to any discussion of the GAO's work.

The TVA was created, as President Roosevelt's legislative message stated, as "a corporation clothed with the power of government but possessed of the flexibility and initiative of a private enterprise." The GAO's first comptroller general, John R. McCarl, who served from 1921 to 1936, saw no reason why TVA should be treated in any special manner by the GAO. The TVA Act of 1933 called for an audit by the GAO, and McCarl sought to make the audit in the same manner as he would make one for any federal department. But because Congress had created the

[17] General Accounting Office, *Annual Report, 1969,* pp. 3–6. Also January 5, 1970, GAO press release on this report.

TVA as a corporate enterprise, it was not analogous to other federal departments. McCarl's goal, therefore, introduced an incompatibility that naturally led to conflict.

Five basic issues divided the GAO and the TVA: (1) GAO demanded that the audit be conducted in its Washington office using fully documented submissions. TVA maintained that a field audit was needed at its principal offices in the South. (2) GAO demanded that TVA's funds be handled through a disbursing officer bonded to be accountable personally to the comptroller general. TVA insisted that its funds, and its responsibility for them, were corporate in nature and that TVA's treasurer was accountable only to the TVA Board of Directors. (3) GAO demanded that TVA operating receipts be transferred to the U.S. Treasury by warrant, and be withdrawn again, along with appropriations, only by warrant. TVA wanted to treat all its funds, receipts, and appropriations alike, as corporate property on special deposit with the U.S. Treasury in a checking account maintained by the TVA treasurer. (4) GAO denied the TVA Board's authority to make such expenditures as those for contracts for construction materials, land, and personal services except in conformity with the comptroller general's interpretation of the statutes usually applicable to other government departments. TVA made it clear that it was prepared to disregard these statutes when they led to serious waste, delay, or inefficiency. (5) GAO undertook to dictate accounting methods for TVA like those prescribed by the Budget and Accounting Act of 1921. TVA also asserted its independence of GAO's control in this field.[18]

The comptroller general, apparently having accepted some of TVA's arguments, sent GAO auditors to Knoxville, Tennessee, early in 1935 for a post-audit of TVA's 1934 operations. The report of this audit consisted mainly of exceptions taken to disbursements totaling over $2 million and of critical comment on TVA's activities and practices. Not only the contents of the report but also its tone made it useful to TVA's enemies. As a result, the

---

[18] An excellent summary account of the GAO-TVA disagreement is contained in Mansfield, *The Comptroller General,* ch. 9, pp. 232–44. The five summary issues listed above are taken from this account.

19

.

TVA Board of Directors was called before the House Military Affairs Committee to discuss the report.

Although the report was critical, it did not make accusations of fraud or misapplication of funds as was charged by some opponents of TVA. Part of the problem, it developed, lay in the fact that TVA had been given no opportunity to comment on the report before it was made public. This fact led to an amendment to the TVA Act stipulating that TVA be allowed to review GAO reports prior to their publication. The amendment also required that the GAO file with the reports any criticisms or comments made by TVA.

In 1935, midway in the act of making a TVA audit in the field, the GAO had to withdraw its auditors because of a lack of funds. So once again it asked TVA to send its vouchers to Washington. TVA complied with this request, but at the same time it reaffirmed its understanding that the TVA Act called for a field audit and also that the GAO had no authority to settle or disallow TVA's disbursements under the Budget and Accounting Act.

During the years immediately following the controversial 1934 report, the GAO sent no reports to Congress on TVA activities. In his annual report to Congress for fiscal year 1937, however, Acting Comptroller General Richard N. Elliot (McCarl's term had ended in mid-1936) stated that the GAO was working on these unreleased TVA reports and that it had taken exception to nearly 8,000 TVA transactions during 1936 and 1937 that totaled $15.5 million. Proper TVA explanation, the report continued, had eliminated about one-third of the exceptions.[19]

The report of the GAO strengthened the efforts of those who were seeking a congressional investigation of the TVA. Later, when this investigation materialized (hearings were held in Knoxville and Washington from spring 1938 to early 1939), the GAO-TVA argument was aired. Thus, TVA's comptroller, E. L. Kohler, was given the opportunity to express his opinion of the GAO and its methods:

[19] Much of this account is taken from C. Herman Pritchett's work, *The Tennessee Valley Authority: A Study in Public Administration* (Chapel Hill: The University of North Carolina Press, 1943), pp. 249–58.

It has long been recognized that the Comptroller General regards himself not as an accountant but as a glorified watchdog, and that he has surrounded himself with a narrow-visioned legal staff that recognizes no superior except a decision of the Supreme Court directly in point. In my opinion, he has more than once been sadly out of line with the spirit of the Budget and Accounting Act of 1921 from which he derives his primary authority . . . .

A review of this report (1934) and frequent contact this year with the field staff, convinced me quickly and decisively that the field staff had made no real audit originally and had made none since; the staff has consisted of persons styled "investigators" who have had little accounting training or experience; and the 1934 report was in no sense an audit report but rather a disorderly miscellany of fact and fancy that could succeed only in misleading the reader, regardless of his skill in auditing, accounting, or sleuthing.[20]

The joint congressional investigating committee concluded that "in the opinion of the committee, the $100,000 spent on General Accounting Office activities (with regard to TVA operations) has produced results largely negative in character. To date, after more than five years of field work, only one audit report has appeared. That report was tentative rather than final, and the bulk of the exceptions taken and criticisms made would have to be abandoned if a final report were to be attempted. As a preliminary account of the operations (of TVA) for 1934, the report succeeded in creating confusion and misconception."[21]

The committee then made some suggestions for GAO operating procedures that, in many ways, pointed to a brighter future. For example, these suggestions helped lay the foundation for the Government Corporation Control Act of 1945 which eventually led to a more comprehensive and effective audit program for all government agencies. The committee recommended (1) that the GAO make periodic commercial audits of TVA in the field and not in Washington, (2) that information on financial, accounting,

[20] U.S., Congress, Joint Committee, *Hearings, Investigations of the Tennessee Valley Authority,* 75th Cong., 3d sess., 1939, Pt. 13, pp. 5897–98.

[21] U.S., Congress, Joint Committee, *Report on the Investigation of the TVA,* 76th Cong., 1st sess., 1939, Senate Doc. No. 56, p. 130.

and management practices be obtained by using auditing experts with a broad and thorough knowledge of corporate procedures, and (3) that emphasis be placed not on individual transactions but on the practices and procedures that produce them.[22]

The second comptroller general of the GAO, former Senator Fred Brown, had been a member of the joint congressional investigating committee, and seemed determined to improve GAO-TVA relations; but ill health forced him to resign after serving little more than a year of his term (April, 1939 to June, 1940). Before his resignation, however, the GAO and the TVA initiated a series of conferences to attempt to settle their differences. The conferences were continued under Brown's successor, former Congressman Lindsay C. Warren (appointed November, 1940), and they resulted in an agreement between GAO and TVA on an amendment to the TVA Act that would remove all differences of opinion on legal and procedural matters. This amendment became law in November, 1941.

As amended, the TVA Act supported the GAO's contention that TVA should render accounts for adjustment and settlement in accordance with the Budget and Accounting Act of 1921. It provided, however, that TVA would be subject only to the provisions of the TVA Act in the conduct of its affairs, and that the GAO could not disallow any expenditure that the TVA Board considered necessary to carry out the provisions of that act. It also allowed TVA to determine its own system of administrative accounts and the form and content of its contracts and other business documents. The audit reports issued subsequent to this amendment showed that the GAO was conducting its field audits along the general lines of those conducted by independent accounting firms.[23]

III

Four years later, Comptroller General Warren and his assistant Frank H. Weitzel, sensing that government corporations,

[22] *Ibid.*, p. 133.
[23] Tennessee Valley Authority, *The Division of Finance of the Tennessee Valley Authority* (Knoxville: Tennessee Valley Authority, 1958), p. 44.

because they were not covered by the work of the GAO, represented a distinct loophole in the congressional supervision of the executive branch, advised Congress of this weakness. The information led to the passage of the Government Corporation Control Act of 1945. The GAO thus played an active role in this legislative milestone and accomplishment; in fact, it drafted part of the basic document. The act directed the comptroller general to make commercial-type, on-site audits of all government corporations and authorized him to settle and adjust the accounts of accountable officers on the basis of such audits. However, the GAO was not given disallowance power. The act also directed the GAO to include in its reports comments and recommendations on the operation and financial condition of the agencies audited.

Government corporations were prohibited from obtaining private audits unless a specific exemption was made by law—a point of special significance for TVA, which had used a private auditor since 1938. In TVA's case the prohibition of this practice lasted until 1959 when bond-financing legislation permitted the Authority to resume its use of private auditors—but in addition to, not in place of, the GAO auditors.

Gerald Schulsinger, in his case study of the GAO, refers to the agency, as it developed under Comptroller General Warren, as "The New GAO." This designation rightly suggests that the GAO was entering a new era. Warren obtained legislation clarifying the interrelationship of the government corporation, the GAO, and Congress; he created (late in 1945) a Corporation Audits Division in the GAO and staffed it with able men (many of whom had been critics of past GAO procedures); he insisted that auditors know the laws, legislative history, purposes, and programs of corporations; and he developed a more business-oriented, or commercial-type, audit.

The commercial-type audit, supported in this case by disallowance power, was expanded in the late 1940s to the noncorporate agencies and became, in effect, the GAO's comprehensive-audit program. Essentially designed to evaluate how well an agency has discharged its financial responsibilities, the comprehensive-audit program includes a study of the agency's programs, procedures, and techniques, and the laws applicable to these activities, in an effort to determine whether the agency has utilized its resources in a legal, efficient, and economical manner. The GAO then makes recommendations for improvement to the agency and to Congress. If, during the GAO's study, disagreements between the agency and the GAO have been resolved, only the resolution appears in the report to Congress. As previously mentioned, the Budgeting and Accounting Procedures Act of 1950 incorporated the refinements begun under Mr. Warren: the comprehensive-audit program and the joint-accounting improvement program.[24]

The improved GAO techniques of today were in part hammered out in the course of the GAO-TVA conflicts. The Government Corporation Control Act of 1945, for example, reflects the resolution of these controversies, and the improved methods written into it are followed by the GAO in all its activities. But rather than conclude that the GAO-TVA feud caused these improvements to be made, it is more accurate to think of the TVA as a vital and energetic partner in making this administrative history.

GAO-TVA relations showed steady improvement from the time Warren began his term in 1940. The first audit of TVA under the Government Corporation Control Act was complimentary:

> In our opinion, TVA's accounts generally are well conceived, supervised, and maintained, and the Authority is to be commended as one of the foremost Government corporations in the use of accounting in management, comparing quite favorably in this respect with well-managed private corporations.
>
> Insofar as we are qualified to make general observations regarding the character of the management of TVA, and insofar as covered within the scope of our audit, we believe that the management is entitled to the highest commendation for the effectiveness with which the Authority functions and for its

---

[24] Gerald G. Schulsinger, *The General Accounting Office: Two Glimpses*, Case No. 35, Inter-University Case Program Series (University, Ala.: University of Alabama Press, 1956), pp. 36–37; U.S., Congress, House, Committee on Goverment Operations, *The General Accounting Office*, pp. 65–69.

accomplishments in carrying out the objectives of the TVA Act . . . .[25]

This favorable atmosphere in GAO-TVA relations continued under Comptroller General Joseph Campbell (December, 1954 to July, 1965) and still continues under his successor, Comptroller General Elmer B. Staats. There have been various differences of opinion, as will be seen in the next chapter, but they, according to officials of both agencies, have been professional differences in judgment rather than personal accusations and counter charges. Although TVA may accept part of the blame for the early disagreements, the impartial observer is forced to conclude that the GAO was obviously suspicious of the struggling new corporation in those early days and that the GAO was also generally rigid and lacking in skill in corporate matters.

[25] General Accounting Office, *GAO Audit Report of the TVA for Fiscal Year 1945* (Washington, D.C.: General Accounting Office, 1947), p. 7.

III. TVA AND THE AUDIT PROCESS

O_F the great number of audit
reports that the GAO issues in any given year (1,023 in 1969),
those concerning TVA operations form only a very small part, yet
it is a most revealing one. Such examples serve to illustrate the
content of the GAO audit reports, the nature of the reporting process, and the various uses Congress makes of the reports. As to the
importance of this audit-reporting aspect of the GAO's work, Robert Wallace, in his *Congressional Control of Federal Spending,*
wrote:

> . . . The General Accounting Office, through its constant contact
> with government operations in the process of investigation and
> the keeping of accounts, and in the issuance of its reports, is
> one of the congressional sources for "leads." The audit reports
> of the GAO are particularly valuable. Tips about examples of
> waste and extravagance as well as maladministration are con-
> stantly received by the committees. Many of these are investi-
> gated prior to the hearings or form the subject of questions at
> the time of an agency's appearance.[1]

The Government Corporation Control Act of 1945 clarified
the authority for the GAO's annual report to Congress on TVA operations. Section 206 of the Legislative Reorganization Act of
1946 extended the GAO's authority by stating that the reports
should contain " . . . such comments and information as may be
deemed necessary to keep Congress informed of the operations
and financial conditions of the several corporations, together with
such recommendations . . . as the Comptroller General may deem
advisable . . . ." This wording authorized the GAO to make "com-

[1] Wallace, *Congressional Control of Federal Spending,* p. 53.

prehensive" audit reports of the TVA and allowed the comptroller general to determine the extent of the comprehensiveness.

The latitude given the GAO is illustrated by the reports for the fiscal years 1957 through 1961, which, as a result of the comptroller general's interpretation of "comprehensive," contain a study of TVA's methods, procedures, programs, and management approaches as well as the more usual audit of the agency's financial transactions. The GAO, that is, was concerned with the proper and "best" use of the funds available to the TVA. By fiscal year 1962 however, the GAO had begun to confine itself primarily to audit reports on TVA's financial statements.

This shift in the auditing procedure in TVA's case was explained, in part, by a GAO official who stated that GAO's auditing schedule is dependent upon several factors, including current congressional interests; the occurrence of unusual events; the availability of manpower in the GAO; and a GAO-established, rule-of-thumb schedule to study in depth certain kinds of governmental activities, or programs, every specified number of years. The GAO's *Annual Report for Fiscal Year 1966,* for example, states, "In selecting areas for audit, we make every effort to include subjects in which we have reason to believe Congress is particularly interested."[2]

There is another factor, however, that has reshaped the auditing approach in recent years. The GAO has been struggling with this basic problem: Given its limited sources and its deadlines, how, in the face of its statutory responsibilities and the expectations of Congress, can the agency most effectively do its job? The GAO seems now to have arrived at a tentative answer to this question and a *modus operandi,* which are reflected in recent audit reports on TVA focusing as they do on the TVA financial statements. At the same time, however, the GAO is conducting research on other relevant TVA problems, the results of which may provide a separate report to Congress at a later date. Thus, the comprehensive-audit program is no longer conceived of as necessarily a

---

[2] General Accounting Office, *Annual Report, 1966,* p. 8.

single, all-encompassing document, but rather as a series of reports examining particular activities and programs.

Although the *1967 Audit Report of TVA,* for example, was merely an examination of TVA's financial statements, the research done at the same time included a comparison of economic-study techniques used by the TVA, the Corps of Engineers, and the Bureau of Reclamation in justifying water-resource projects; a comparison of construction costs for a new TVA building at Chattanooga, Tennessee, with those for similar buildings of other government agencies; and a review of TVA's coal-procurement practices in the light of its nuclear-power plant and nuclear-fuel contracts. Findings and comments on these matters may show up in later special reports to Congress.[3]

In addition to the annual-audit reports for the period 1957–68, five other GAO reports on TVA activities were especially requested by Congress: one to the Senate Committee on Public Works concerning bills to provide for the expansion of TVA's power system by the sale of bonds to the public (1957); another, to the House Committee on Government Operations, on a bill to provide for a survey of TVA's fertilizer operations (1957); a third, to the Senate Committee on Public Works, concerning a bill to provide for prior congressional approval of TVA's use of its power revenues for the construction or acquisition of additional power-producing units and facilities (1957); a fourth, to the House Committee on Government Operations, on TVA's urgent-purchases procedures (1962); and the fifth, a report to the whole Congress—not specifically on TVA, but of direct interest to it—dealing with the sale of hydroelectric power by the Department of the Interior to TVA at rates specifically disapproved by the Federal Power Commission (1964). Further, the GAO annual reports during this period often stated that other more informal reports were made to individual members of Congress on matters pertaining to TVA. For example, in 1964 such a report was made to a senator on TVA's sales of electric power. Also, two GAO reports were sent only to the TVA, one dealing with TVA's coal-procurement practices

---

[3] Interviews with GAO and TVA officials.

(1957), the second dealing with TVA's fertilizer program (1959). Although these special reports were available to Congress, they seemed to be of significant interest only to TVA.[4]

I

A better perspective on the specific subjects covered and questions raised in the GAO's reports can be gained by examining some of the findings presented to Congress from 1957 through 1968. The examples cited are from audits made at TVA centers in Knoxville, Tennessee; Chattanooga, Tennessee; and Wilson Dam, Alabama; as well as at various power and construction project sites in the Tennessee Valley. They are presented here in two groups: first, those intended only to provide information for Congress, and second, those that involved controversy or disagreement between the two agencies. Where applicable, a brief mention is made of any significant action that followed the GAO reports:[5]

1. Audit reports informed Congress of TVA's first few payments into the U.S. Treasury of (a) a return (interest) on the government's net appropriation investment in TVA power facilities and (b) a repayment of that investment, as required by TVA's 1959 bond-financing legislation. Information was also provided on the principal features of issues of bonds sold under this legislation. No differences of opinion between the GAO and TVA were apparent.

2. In its audit report for fiscal year 1961, the GAO chose to comment on TVA's policies and procedures for the land-acquisition program for the Melton Hill Dam and Reservoir project near Knoxville, Tennessee, the first reservoir that had been constructed by TVA since 1953. The GAO concluded that TVA's practices for determining compensation to landowners were adequate and rea-

---

[4] Data taken from appendixes to the annual reports of the GAO for the 1957–68 period.

[5] Information compiled from two sources: the GAO's audit reports of TVA for fiscal years 1957–68; and the GAO's annual reports to Congress for fiscal years 1957–68. The issues presented here often stretched across a period of two or three years of reporting. No attempt is made to go into detail. In some cases, however, more detail will be provided later.

sonable. Subsequently, the GAO was consulted, but not directly involved, in a congressional hearing on TVA land-buying policies and procedures, held in Knoxville in the summer of 1963. One of the first of a series of recommendations made by the committee conducting the study (Select Committee on Real Property Acquisition of the Committee on Public Works) was that Congress establish a uniform policy to guide the land-acquisition practices of all federal agencies. Later, in 1968, Congress did legislate a change in TVA's land-acquisition procedures, to bring them into conformity with those of other federal agencies. The extent of congressional reliance on GAO advice on this issue is not known. GAO's earlier investigation, however, did provide some basic information for the congressional action.[6]

3. Other audit reports presented a review, by GAO traffic and transportation specialists, of TVA's traffic operations on the Tennessee River system. The reports covered TVA's negotiations with barge lines for reduced shipping rates and discussed the Authority's efforts to verify the accuracy of carriers' bills to shippers. GAO concluded that TVA's river traffic operations were being run efficiently and economically.

4. The GAO reported that TVA was having serious problems, involving financial damages, in connection with the installation and operation of fourteen Westinghouse turbogenerator units, costing about $46 million. The implication was that TVA should seek settlement from Westinghouse for agency losses. Although the GAO report had little to do with TVA's action in obtaining a damage settlement, it did alert Congress to the problem of identical bid submissions by private firms, which led to subsequent prosecution by the Department of Justice.

5. Congress learned, from the GAO audit reports, of TVA's de-

[6] See U.S., House, Committee on Public Works: (1) *Hearings, Real Property Acquisition Practices,* 88th Cong., 1st sess., 1963; (2) *Study of Compensation and Assistance for Persons Affected by Real Property Acquisition in Federal and Federally Assisted Programs,* 88th Cong., 2nd sess., 1964, Committee Print No. 31; and (3) *TVA—Trial by Jury,* 90th Cong., 2nd sess., 1968, Rept. 1840; and U.S., Tennessee Valley Authority, *Land Acquisition in TVA* (Chattanooga, 1963).

cision to build its first nuclear-power plant, a significant program change for TVA.

6. The GAO reported to Congress on the failure and collapse of a part of TVA's Wheeler Lock, adjacent to the construction area for a new lock. The report provided information on the reasons for the failure, reconstruction work schedules and costs, and temporary facilities provided to maintain the flow of river traffic.

Turning to the areas of disagreement between the two agencies, again as shown by the sampling of 1957–68 records, it will be noted that the issues ranged widely and in some instances are still unresolved. They involve procurement and bidding practices, methods of financial reporting, organizational matters, problems of congressional control, and relations with public and private bodies. In all cases, of course, the GAO's informational role is ever-present and important even when obscured by the conflict arising from its recommendations.

1. The GAO analyzed and criticized a TVA procurement policy regarding purchases of urgently-needed supplies or services—a policy enabling TVA to bypass competitive bidding. This issue became the subject of a congressional hearing held in Washington in January, 1962, which resulted in a clarification of, but no basic change in, the procurement policy.

2. TVA was continuing to purchase power at special low rates from the Southeastern Power Administration (SEPA), which distributed hydroelectric power produced at the Corps of Engineers' projects in Kentucky's Cumberland River Basin, even though such rates had been specifically disapproved by the Federal Power Commission. There was a possibility, therefore, that TVA might be forced to pay a higher rate retroactively. Because the Authority failed to disclose this possible financial liability, the GAO reported that TVA's financial position was not being fairly presented. Several years of disagreement over this subject between the GAO and TVA were ended when the Federal Power Commission finally approved the low rates. Even so, the larger issue, regarding the validity of FPC rulings on power rates, is still in

question, and the GAO has recommended legislation that would give FPC unquestioned authority in these matters.

3. The GAO recommended that TVA discontinue the use of preferential specifications when it invited private coal companies to bid on large quantities of coal, except where a definite monetary value could be assigned to such preferences. These preferences related to such requirements as the dates and schedule of coal delivery and the sources of supply, all without allowance for special compensation by TVA. Preferences that could not be assigned a definite monetary value were either to be made specific requirements of the bid, or to be identified as factors that would not be considered in an award except where bids were equal in all other material respects. The purpose of this GAO recommendation was to enable each prospective bidder to determine in advance the effect on his bid price of any departure in his bid from preferences stated in the invitation. The GAO also reported that TVA's procurement practices for spot coal (surplus coal periodically offered for sale by mines that have produced more coal than they need to fill their long-term contracts) generally did not conform to normal government practice and were also an exception to TVA's normal procurement practice. In response to the GAO's findings, TVA at first assigned specific values to the preferences included in its term-coal (coal purchased under long-term contract) bid invitations. Later, however, this practice was discontinued when TVA ceased to consider such preferences except in cases where differences in bids were slight.

4. Some phases of TVA's agricultural program were conducted by its Division of Agricultural Relations in Knoxville, Tennessee, while others, notably the fertilizer experimentation and production activities, were conducted by its Office of Chemical Engineering at Wilson Dam, Alabama. The GAO recommended that the former be moved from Knoxville to Wilson Dam and that the administrative functions of the two divisions be combined under a single administrative head. TVA stated that this very consolidation was already under consideration and that a report on it by the GAO was therefore unnecessary. The consolidation was eventually effected.

5. The GAO recommended that the TVA and the U.S. Department of Agriculture (USDA) negotiate a formal understanding about areas of responsibility in regard to certain agricultural programs of the Authority that were clearly related to those of the department. Both TVA and the USDA concluded that a formal understanding was unnecessary, but they did agree informally on a number of operating principles designed to encourage closer coordination at the field level.

6. The GAO recommended that TVA reexamine the rate it charged for power sold to the Atomic Energy Commission (AEC), its largest customer, in relation to the rate it charged other customers. The implication was that the government was being overcharged. When TVA made a study of its rates, the GAO's position was partly upheld, but TVA asserted that the study techniques prescribed by the GAO were not valid and the results, therefore, were meaningless. Although TVA was questioned about this point at congressional appropriations hearings, no change was made in TVA's power rates.

7. TVA's power program is now financed by the sale of bonds and by revenues from the sale of power; other TVA programs are financed largely by appropriations. Shortly after the 1959 bond amendment, TVA experimented with combining these two facets —power funds and appropriations—into a single financial statement; but the GAO recommended that the power program be treated separately in the financial reports. The recommendation was accepted by TVA.

8. Prior to passage of the legislation allowing TVA to finance future additions to its power system by selling revenue bonds, the GAO had urged that Congress retain its control over these expenditures by appropriating the necessary funds for new steam-generating units. However, if Congress were willing to allow TVA to use funds from sources other than appropriations for this purpose, the Authority, GAO held, should at least be required to obtain specific and prior authority from Congress. In addition, the GAO consistently recommended that TVA be directed to pay interest on the government's investment in the power program and that, if necessary for the sound conduct of the power pro-

33

gram, the financial pay-back schedule to the Treasury should be modified. The GAO lost its main argument with the passage, in August, 1959, of the self-financing legislation. However, the legislation also required TVA to repay, on a new and more stringent schedule, a return (interest) on the government's earlier appropriations investment in TVA's power program, as well as to repay the investment itself. Thus, the GAO's long-held position on this latter point was put into effect.

The foregoing examples are only a small sampling of interesting and significant items in the GAO reports for this period. But they are quite representative samples, and they reflect the nature and variety of GAO-TVA discussions. Also, they show that some issues are settled privately between the GAO and the TVA, some require congressional involvement, and some are never settled.

Some of these issues were critically important to the two agencies and each quite naturally saw them in a different light. For example, TVA viewed the power-financing legislation as basic to the Authority's continued existence, and not without good reason: TVA's future did indeed look dim during the Eisenhower years and the Dixon-Yates episode.[7] On the other hand, the GAO, as Congress's employee, saw a weakening of congressional control in TVA's desire to finance capital additions through the sale of bonds rather than by appropriations. Similarly, the GAO's opposition to TVA purchases of power at rates disapproved by the Federal Power Commission was only part of its larger campaign "to get the finances and procedures of the power and resource development agencies in shape."[8]

[7] Aaron Wildavsky, *Dixon-Yates: A Study in Power Politics* (New Haven and London: Yale University Press, 1962), especially ch. 18. "Dixon-Yates" refers to an important public *v.* private power skirmish which occurred in the early 1950s when the Eisenhower administration promoted a complex arrangement to, in effect, prevent TVA from constructing additional power facilities—a private power plant was to be built under a contract with the Atomic Energy Commission to supply power to TVA's Memphis, Tennessee, service area.

[8] General Accounting Office, *Report to the Congress: Sale of Hydroelectric Power by the Department of The Interior Under Section 5 of the Flood Control Act of 1944 at Rates Not Approved by the Federal Power Commission* (Washington, D.C., 1964). Also, interviews with GAO officials.

Several of the issues were highly significant on the basis of dollars alone. TVA's negotiated purchases (those that bypassed the bid process) rose from $2,203,000 in fiscal year 1955 to $7,-486,000 in fiscal year 1961, a substantial amount although only 6 percent to 7 percent of TVA's total purchases of manufactured items for those years.[9] Furthermore, since TVA in fiscal year 1957 awarded contracts for coal valued at $97.7 million, its coal-procurement activity was big business. Clearly, then, the GAO's charges that "the procedure followed . . . does not comply with the requirements of the TVA Act" and that "the procurement practices . . . do not conform to normal Government procurement practices . . . " were meant to draw attention to a legitimate area of concern.[10] Similarly, when the GAO recommended a consolidation of TVA's agricultural and chemical operations and called for closer TVA cooperation with the U.S. Department of Agriculture, it was touching on activities that involve large funds, both in appropriations and in revenue. For fiscal year 1968, the actual financing for the Office of Agriculture and Chemical Development, which reaches into virtually every state in the nation, was roughly $10.6 million in appropriations and $19.1 million in revenues.[11] With reference to funds involved in the TVA purchase of power from the Department of the Interior at low, FPC-disapproved rates, the GAO reported that "About $12.6 million in additional revenues would have been collected from the Tennessee Valley Authority over the past fifteen years if rates conforming to the criteria contemplated by the Federal Power Commission had been in effect."[12]

II

The fact that the GAO is indispensible to Congress as a source of information calls for a closer look at the details of how the

[9] TVA staff study, "TVA Negotiated Purchases—Fiscal Years 1955, 1958, and 1961," Sept. 27, 1961.

[10] General Accounting Office, *GAO Audit Report, 1957,* pp. 85–87; see also *GAO Audit Report, 1958.*

[11] Tennessee Valley Authority, *Budget Program for Fiscal Year 1970* (Knoxville, 1969), beginning summary statements.

[12] General Accounting Office, *Sale of Hydroelectric Power,* p. 1.

audit process is carried out and how the reports are put together. In the GAO-TVA relationship, there is an added feature in the form of an annual audit performed for TVA by a private accounting firm.[13]

The New York accounting firm of Lybrand, Ross Bros., and Montgomery is employed by TVA. Every year the accountants spend about three weeks in June, prior to the close of the fiscal year, gathering preliminary data at TVA, and then return for most of August to check their earlier findings. The firm's short-form certification of TVA's financial statements is generally available at the end of August or early in September.[14] *GAO's Audit Report of TVA for Fiscal Year 1966* states that, as provided by the 1959 amendment to the TVA Act (the bond-financing legislation), TVA is not restricted by the Government Corporation Control Act and is therefore empowered to employ a firm of certified public accountants to facilitate the Authority's issuance and sale of revenue bonds. This report continues:

> The audit by the firm of certified public accountants does not take the place of that required by our Office under the Government Corporation Control Act. However, in view of the fact that a firm of certified public accountants was employed by the Authority, our audit included observations and tests of the firm's audit work.
>
> The financial statements and supporting schedules prepared by the Authority are incorporated in this report together with the opinion of the firm of certified public accountants employed by the Authority.

The GAO customarily sends four employees from its Atlanta regional office to carry out TVA's audit. These employees perform their work largely in conjunction with that of the private auditors. The GAO crew usually consists of a part-time supervisor and three other auditors, working chiefly at Knoxville and Chattanooga, Tennessee, and Wilson Dam, Alabama. Concerning the usefulness of the GAO reports, TVA officials interviewed felt that the long-form audit reports (the single comprehensive documents),

[13] Andrew F. McCall and Zane Geier, "A Teamwork Venture with Public Accountants in the Audit of TVA," *GAO Review* (Winter, 1968).
[14] Interviews with TVA officials.

the type prepared by the GAO in the earlier days, were too late to be of use to TVA in preparing its annual reports to the President and Congress, even though they often were issued early enough to meet the statutory requirements of the Corporation Control Act. They also stated that the reports were both too late and in the wrong form to meet the needs of business interests in the bond market seeking information about TVA and its power program. The same TVA officials conceded, however, that the GAO's new approach of issuing short-form financial reports, supplemented if necessary by later special reports, eliminated many of these objections since at least draft reports were available much earlier.[15]

The short-form audit report for TVA was first introduced by the GAO in anticipation of the passage of TVA's bond-financing legislation in 1959. Thinking that this new form, submitted early in October, would serve TVA's needs in selling bonds under the new legislation, the GAO prepared such reports for fiscal years 1958 and 1959 in addition to making its usual comprehensive reports for those years. GAO officials said that they were willing to discuss their findings with investment houses and felt that their audits would be acceptable to investors. TVA, however, while not doubting GAO's competence, felt that investors knew little about the GAO and were inclined to look upon it as "just another part of the government." The ultimate agreement was to use both the government and the private audits, but to minimize duplication between them. TVA feared the possibility that the GAO audits might contain statements casting doubt on the lawfulness or wisdom of some aspect of TVA operations, which would cause difficulties in selling an issue of bonds if the GAO opinion were not counterbalanced by the private firm's report.[16] After two years of using both reports, both GAO and TVA agreed that the coordination was working well and should be continued.

Meetings at which GAO and TVA discussed the issues to be in-

[15] See the earlier discussion in this chapter for further details on the revised audit approach of the GAO.

[16] Notes from TVA files on meetings between GAO and TVA officials, held Oct. 28, 1959, and Nov. 17, 1961, regarding *GAO Audit Report, 1959* and *GAO Audit Report, 1961*, respectively.

cluded in the audit reports provide an interesting insight into the audit (and the administrative) process. Quite often, a spirit of cooperation seemed to develop at these meetings, with each party giving sympathetic consideration to the other's needs. For instance, at a meeting concerning the deficiencies of the Westinghouse generator units purchased by TVA (mentioned earlier in this chapter), GAO felt that the matter should be reported to Congress and asked TVA's advice about the best procedure. TVA requested that the information be presented in general terms, merely indicating the nature of the problem but not, at that point, including estimates of the damage or referring to the pioneering and experimental nature of TVA's work in this area of new, larger-capacity generating units. TVA thought that a report in broad, general terms would avoid possible injury to its position in any future litigation or settlement. The GAO complied with TVA's wishes in its 1957 report.

The GAO, however, is not always so agreeable. Following the cost study of TVA power supplied to the AEC—the study that showed that TVA charged the AEC more than it did many other customers—the GAO said that reference to the study would be made in its audit report and asked for TVA's comments. TVA complied, and its reservations were included in the audit report. As will be seen in the next chapter, TVA was later questioned on this point at appropriations hearings.

In the discussion of TVA's urgent-purchases procedure at a 1961 meeting, the GAO was again not very agreeable. Despite TVA's efforts to justify its procedure, GAO felt that TVA should be required to have specific statutory authority for making such purchases. The GAO made it clear that its position would be stated and advocated in its forthcoming report.[17] This disagreement eventually led to a hearing before a subcommittee of the House Committee on Government Operations.

Such meetings, of course, do not always settle the issues discussed or end the GAO-TVA dialogue about them. Occasionally,

---

[17] Information taken from TVA files, *ibid.* Also, notes from TVA files on a meeting between GAO and TVA officials, held Nov. 1, 1957, regarding *GAO Audit Report, 1957.*

the firm positions on both sides become apparent only after the conferences are concluded. The post-meeting procedure is generally as follows: In early December, GAO asks TVA by letter to comment on the first draft of its audit report. The GAO may or may not alter its report on the basis of TVA's comments. The point is finally reached at which neither side can, or will, make further concessions. A statement in an internal TVA paper of 1958 characterizes this point of final and fixed positions: " . . . GAO would meet with us to discuss these matters further if we insisted but we had serious doubts that anything could be accomplished by such a meeting."[18] The time invariably arrives, of course, for the polite exchanges. GAO to TVA: "I would like to take this opportunity to express my Office's appreciation for TVA's interest . . . and particularly for the efforts of your staff in expeditiously furnishing TVA's views." Then, TVA to GAO: "We would like to express our appreciation to you and your associates for the trouble you have taken to see to it that TVA's views are properly reflected."[19]

[18] Memorandum, in the files of TVA, dated Jan. 6, 1959, regarding *GAO Audit Report, 1958*.
[19] Letters, in the files of TVA, between GAO and TVA officials, dated Jan. 30, 1958, and Feb. 10, 1958, regarding *GAO Audit Report, 1957*.

T HE GAO maintains a steady flow of information to Congress in the form of audits and other reports on the various governmental agencies. Some of the reports are periodic in nature as required by law, others are prepared in response to specific congressional or agency requests, and still others are developed by the GAO on its own initiative in anticipation of congressional requirements. Thus, the present pattern of reporting represents an evolvement based on both law and need.

In its distribution of the reports, the GAO sends those of broader interest to Congress as a whole. Here again, such distribution is in some cases set by law, but other reports reach the entire Congress if they contain recommendations for legislative action or if they are considered to be of concern or use to the total body or to several of its committees. Addressed to the president of the Senate and the speaker of the House, these reports are produced in multiple copies and distributed widely. Copies go to the Treasury Department, the Bureau of the Budget, the Senate and House committees on appropriations, the Senate and House committees on government operations, the appropriate legislative committees in the House and Senate, members of Congress from districts in which the reported activities are located, the agencies involved, and to still others as requested by Congress or as appropriate to the subject matter of the report.

As might be expected, the reports of a more restricted nature receive only a limited distribution. If a specific congressional committee requests audit work or other data, or if the subject matter of a report pertains solely to a single committee, only that committee receives the report. A similarly limited distribution is made in the case of reports to government agencies, especially if the reports do not require congressional action and appear to be of little concern to Congress.[1]

Although major reports of the GAO are addressed to the respective leaders of the Senate and the House, the agency's basic links with Congress are the committees on government operations of the two houses. Authority for this informational channel resides in the Legislative Reorganization Act of 1946 previously discussed, and the two committees list among their formal powers and duties the "receiving and examining reports of the Comptroller General of the United States and of submitting such recommendations to the House or [Senate] as deemed necessary or desirable in connection with the subject matter of such reports."

Hardly less important than this close liaison, however, are the GAO's service ties to the appropriations and legislative committees of both houses. Aware of the dispersed nature of power, influence, and responsibility in Congress, the GAO makes a special effort to meet the needs of these committees in both Senate and House. Authority for this GAO function, as well as for service to Congress as a whole, dates back to the 1921 Budget and Accounting Act. This act states that the comptroller general must make investigations and reports as ordered by either house of Congress or by any committee having jurisdiction over revenue, appropriations, or expenditures, and must furnish these committees with any aid or information requested. Section 206 of the Legislative Reorganization Act of 1946 reinforced this many-faceted responsibility of the GAO:

> The Comptroller General is authorized and directed to make an expenditure analysis of each agency in the executive branch of the Government (including Government corporations), which in the opinion of the Comptroller General, will enable Congress to determine whether public funds have been econom-

[1] U.S., Congress, Senate, Committee on Government Operations, *Review of Audit Reports of the Comptroller General,* 84th Cong., 2nd sess., 1956, Rept. 1572, p. 23; and General Accounting Office, *Annual Report, 1967,* p. 173 n.2.

ically and efficiently administered and expended. Reports on such analyses shall be submitted by the Comptroller General, from time to time, to the Committees on Government Operations, to the Appropriations Committees and to the legislative committees having jurisdiction over legislation relating to the operations of the respective agencies, of the two Houses.[2]

I

As the prime receivers of the GAO reports, the House and Senate committees on government operations differ markedly in their handling of these reports. Like many other congressional committees with overlapping responsibilities, the two groups have evolved a working arrangement that diminishes the problem of duplication inherent in Congress's dual committee system. In general, the House committee uses GAO findings to study government efficiency, effectiveness, and compliance with congressional intent; the Senate committee, on the other hand, is primarily interested in whatever aid the GAO might provide to help the committee in its investigations of possible law violations or improper use of federal funds or property. Exceptions are not uncommon, however, to this necessarily generalized view of the differing approaches of the two committees.

When a GAO audit report reaches the House committee, it goes to the committee's Associate General Counsel for a brief review and assignment to the appropriate subcommittee for follow-up. The subcommittee then gives the agency under study thirty days in which to comment on the issues contained in the report. A full record of these transactions is maintained, the various subcommittees making periodic reports to the chairman of the full committee on the status of the reports and action taken, and the whole being incorporated in the annual activity report of the committee.[3]

[2] U.S., Congress, Senate, Committee on Government Operations, *Legislative Calendar,* 90th Cong., 1st sess., Nov. 4, 1967, pp. 5–8; and House, Committee on Government Operations, *Legislative Calendar,* 90th Cong., 1st sess., Dec. 28, 1967, pp. 4–6.

[3] Interviews in Washington, D.C., with professional staff members of the House Committee on Government Operations. See also, U.S., Con-

A closer look at follow-up action by the House committee can be gained by taking an example from TVA history. Although TVA's affairs in the House are currently the responsibility of the Natural Resources and Power Subcommittee of the Committee on Government Operations, prior to 1963 the Authority was under the Executive and Legislative Reorganization Subcommittee. Records of that earlier period indicate that the follow-up was pursued with consistency. Congressman William L. Dawson (Democrat, Illinois) was not only chairman of the Committee on Government Operations but was also head of the subcommittee then handling TVA affairs, and he apparently demanded careful follow-up on all GAO reports. TVA files provide substantial evidence to this effect: letters to TVA from the subcommittee raised questions on every audit report that contained critical comment by the GAO. One such exchange, relating to TVA's urgent purchases policy (*Audit Report for Fiscal Year 1960*), led to a hearing before the subcommittee on January 25, 1962. The correspondence, including several letters from TVA to the subcommittee, indicates that TVA's written explanation and comments on the issue failed to satisfy the subcommittee members, and a hearing on the issue was called.[4]

In contrast to this rather close follow-up by the House committee, the Senate Committee on Government Operations tends to be more selective in its attention to the GAO reports. As previously mentioned, the Senate body is generally most interested in those reports that reflect a possible violation of law or an improper use of federal funds or property. Such reports are

---

gress, House, Committee on Government Operations, *Activities of the House Committee on Government Operations, 88th Congress,* 89th Cong., 1st sess., 1965, p. 113. According to Bureau of the Budget Cir. No. A–50, an agency has sixty days to explain to the bureau issues contained in GAO audit reports. General Accounting Office, *Annual Report, 1958,* p. 141, touches on the interplay between the Bureau of the Budget and the GAO: "Representatives of the Bureau of the Budget met with us to discuss certain comments of particular interest to them in the report [that is, the General Accounting Office, *Audit Report of TVA, 1957*]."

[4] Letters, in the files of TVA, on the urgent-purchases policy of TVA, between Chairman Dawson and TVA, dated Apr. 12, 1961, through Jan. 23, 1962. Similar exchanges on other issues were also found.

immediately referred to the permanent Subcommittee on Investigations, and each year the GAO assigns a number of its professional personnel to that committee to assist with these and other investigations. The investigative studies have ranged from inquiries into labor-management matters to problems associated with development and procurement of the F111 (TFX) airplane.[5] But the Senate's use of and follow-up on the GAO's work are clearly more limited than that of the House committee which, like the House Appropriations Committee in money matters, seeks more careful mastery of the intricacies and workings of executive operations and programs. Whereas the House committee channels each GAO audit report to the appropriate subcommittee, the Senate committee explains its treatment of these reports as follows:

> These reports were reviewed by the staff of the Committee and, if warranted, by the Senate Permanent Subcommittee on Investigations . . . . Unless some specific action was suggested by the Comptroller General, the Committee took no action on these reports. In some instances, however, other committees having direct oversight jurisdiction over the subject covered by the reports have developed additional information . . . .[6]

This difference in approach of the House and Senate committees can be explained in part by the disparity in the total workload of the individual congressmen serving as committee members. Senators and congressmen are, of course, subject to assignment to subcommittees of the government operations committees, as well as to other committees of Congress. In the House, for instance, the subcommittee structure of the Committee on Government Operations in the Ninetieth Congress (1967–68) included special studies, military operations, government activities, intergovernmental relations, executive and legislative reorganization, natural resources and power, foreign operations and

---

[5] The Senate Committee on Government Operations has also published two excellent reports dealing with the work of the GAO: *Review of Audit Reports of the Comptroller General* (Senate Rept. 1572) and *Financial Management.*

[6] U.S., Congress, Senate, Committee on Government Operations, *Activities of the Senate Committee on Government Operations, 88th Congress,* 89th Cong., 1st sess., 1965, Rept. 69, p. 9.

government information, legal and monetary affairs, and research and technical programs. On the Senate side there were subcommittees on investigations, national security and international operations, intergovernmental relations, executive reorganization, foreign aid expenditures, and government research.[7] Despite the smaller number of Senate subcommittees, the senators in this instance, as is true generally in Congress, held more subcommittee assignments than did government operations committeemen in the House—by virtue of the fact that the Senate Committee on Government Operations was composed of only fifteen members, whereas the House committee was made up of thirty-five members. As for service on other congressional committees, members of the House Committee on Government Operations in the Ninetieth Congress had no more than one other committee assignment, whereas most of their counterparts in the Senate served on two other committees, and a few were assigned to three others. Each of these other committee assignments, in turn, involved additional subcommittee participation for all congressmen.[8] Thus,

[7] U.S., Congress, Senate, Committee on Government Operations, *Legislative Calendar*, pp. 2–4; U.S., Congress, House, Committee on Government Operations, *Interim Report for the House Committee*, 90th Cong., 2nd sess., Feb. 5, 1968.

[8] Interviews in Washington, D.C., with GAO officials and with staff members of the House and Senate committees on government operations; and analysis of "Lists of Standing Committees and Committee Assignments of Senators and Members of the House of Representatives," 90th Cong., by the printing clerk of the Senate and the clerk of the House. Concerning subcommittee assignments for the members of the House and Senate committees on government operations, a brief analysis was made of the two committees' legislative calendars for the 90th Cong. (see n.2 above). According to the rules of the Senate Committee on Government Operations, fifteen senators formed its membership in the 90th Cong. These senators—ten majority, five minority—in turn made up the committee's six subcommittees. There was a total of thirty-three majority assignments and seventeen minority assignments to these subcommittees. Each majority member, therefore, had an average of 3.3 subcommittee assignments, while each minority member had an average of 3.4 assignments.

On the other hand, the ten subcommittees of the House Committee on Government Operations were composed of thirty-five members—twenty majority and fifteen minority. And in this case the thirty-eight majority and twenty-eight minority subcommittee assignments reflected that, on the average, both majority and minority members held only 1.9

the pressure of time and other responsibilities probably forces the Senate committee to restrict its attention to the more critical issues; it is also possible that senatorial awareness of the uniform and meticulous follow-up by the House committee works toward the same result. As one staff member of the House committee put it, matter-of-factly, "the interests and approaches of the two committees are different, and we keep in close touch."

Although congressmen make frequent informal use of the GAO, requesting reports or specific information by telephone or in person, these exchanges are seldom made a matter of record. In the formal congressional hearings, however, a clear record is made of references to the GAO reports, indicating both the nature and the extent of Congress's reliance on the auditing agency. Most of the hearings pertain to legislative or appropriations matters, but the House Committee on Government Operations itself also uses the hearing device to study other subjects brought to its attention by the GAO audits. A 1961 study by the Senate Committee on Government Operations called particular attention to GAO contributions in the legislative and appropriation areas:

> The value of the General Accounting Office reports is reflected in their use by the Congress and its committees. The hearings of the Appropriations Committees contain many references to the findings contained in the audit reports. Legislative Committees have utilized the information and recommendations contained in the reports in considering new and amendatory legislation governing the operations and programs of departments and agencies.[9]

II

The use of the reports in legislative committee hearings is especially well illustrated by the skirmish in the late 1950s over TVA's proposed power-financing legislation. Joseph Harris, in his

---

assignments. Thus, even within the respective Committee on Government Operations, senators have numerically more subcommittee assignments than do congressmen.

[9] U.S., Congress, Senate, *Review of Audit Reports*, p. 26.

Congressional Control of Administration, described the problem and the GAO's position as follows:

> In 1955, and for several years following, the audit reports on the Tennessee Valley Authority included statements in opposition to legislation then being proposed which would authorize TVA to sell revenue bonds to finance construction of steam plants and other power facilities . . . . Thus the Comptroller General stepped into a policy matter that did not involve probity in the use of funds, or even administrative efficiency, but did involve him in a highly political public-private power controversy. However, he takes the position that any diminution of regular annual congressional control of funds is his business to oppose, regardless of the broader policy objectives involved.[10]

Hearings were held in April and June of 1957, by the Subcommittee on Flood Control—Rivers and Harbors of the Senate Committee on Public Works on four bills proposing to amend the TVA Act to provide for the necessary self-financing arrangements. No GAO representative was present at the hearing, but three letters from Comptroller General Joseph Campbell to Senator Dennis Chavez (Democrat, New Mexico), chairman of the public works committee, were included in the record. The letters provided the GAO's analyses of the bills, its comments and recommendations, and repeated the GAO's consistent stand on self-financing through the sale of revenue bonds:

> Our position then, as now, was that the financing of Government activities of this character should be by appropriations . . . . This language would grant practically unlimited authority to TVA in the expansion of its power program. We do not believe that any Government agency should be granted such freedom from the normal controls exercised over governmental activities.[11]

At one point in the hearing, Senator Lister Hill (Democrat, Alabama), not a committee member but appearing as a witness, attempted to assure the subcommittee that this legislation, con-

[10] Joseph P. Harris, *Congressional Control of Administration* (Washington, D.C.: Brookings Institution, 1964), p. 150. Used by permission.
[11] U.S., Congress, Senate, Committee on Public Works, *Hearings, Amending the TVA Act,* 85th Cong., 1st sess., 1957, pp. 12–13.

trary to the GAO position, would not remove TVA from necessary congressional supervision:

> And, of course, the General Accounting Office, an agency of Congress, will continue to perform its "watchdog" audits of TVA finances. It seems to me that the prerogatives of Congress would be fully guarded in this proposed legislation.[12]

Meanwhile, the House was holding its own hearings on the issue, conducted during the spring of 1957 by the Subcommittee on Flood Control of the House Committee on Public Works. At one point, the president of a private power company, appearing on behalf of the U.S. Chamber of Commerce, raised the question of loss of congressional control over TVA's activities and cited the relevant views of the GAO.[13] On hearing this, Congressman Robert E. Jones (Democrat, Alabama) interjected: "Is that the same Mr. Campbell [then GAO's comptroller general] who used to be with the Atomic Energy Commission, which consummated the Dixon-Yates transaction for the AEC?" When the witness responded, "I do not know," Congressman Jones concluded, "I see. Thank you." Congressman Clifford Davis (Democrat, Tennessee), subcommittee chairman, added: "Well, we have heard this philosophy . . . expressed before."[14]

The hearings were continued in the Eighty-sixth Congress, and the GAO's stand now came to be used in hearings even more by congressmen and others. In hearings held in March, 1959, by the House Committee on Public Works, the views of the GAO were repeated by private power and Chamber of Commerce witnesses, this time joined by representatives of the coal industry and other affected interests. Specific references were cited from

[12] *Ibid.,* p. 64.

[13] This particular witness referred to GAO's positions again and again during the course of his testimony.

[14] U.S., Congress, House, Subcommittee on Flood Control of the House Committee on Public Works, *Hearings, Tennessee Valley Authority Financing,* 85th Cong., 1st sess., 1957, pp. 225, 246–47. The fact is that Comptroller General Joseph Campbell, while a member of the AEC, had voted for the Dixon-Yates contract. It should also be noted, however, that when the question of the settlement of the Dixon-Yates claim against the government came before the GAO, Comptroller General Campbell forced the claim to the Supreme Court, where it was rejected.

GAO audit reports of TVA.[15] Although the hearing pertained to TVA financing, it is interesting to note that Congressman Fred Schwengel, Jr. (Republican, Iowa) apparently used GAO data also to query TVA representatives on a different subject. Without even mentioning the GAO's recent concern over TVA's coal-buying practices, he proceeded to question at length, and quite critically, TVA's record on this matter, using facts and figures identical to those appearing in GAO audit reports.[16]

The Senate Committee on Public Works held a final hearing on the revenue-bond issue in June, 1959. Senator Lister Hill again referred to the GAO as a device by which Congress could check on TVA's increased freedom under the proposed new legislation, and the committee again recorded a letter from Comptroller General Campbell reaffirming GAO's opposition to such potential loss of congressional control. At this hearing, however, the committee also heard from three other officials of the GAO, welcomed by Senator Robert Kerr (Democrat, Oklahoma), chairman of the flood control subcommittee, as "this distinguished group." The GAO spokesmen essentially reiterated the agency's position and commented on various parts of the pending bills. No questions were asked of them.[17]

III

In the case of appropriations hearings, the Senate apparently makes only moderate direct use of the GAO reports as compared with the House. A careful examination of TVA's hearings before the Senate Subcommittee on Public Works Appropriations for recent congresses disclosed not a single reference to the GAO's audits of TVA. Significantly, however, several of the issues raised

[15] U.S., Congress, House, Committee on Public Works, *Hearings, Tennessee Valley Authority,* 86th Cong., 1st sess., 1959, pp. 178, 186, 191, and 204.

[16] The bulk of Congressman Schwengel's comments and TVA's responses are on pp. 27–34 of the hearing transcript.

[17] U.S., Congress, Senate, Committee on Public Works, *Hearings, Revenue Bond Financing by TVA,* 86th Cong., 1st sess., 1959, pp. 26, 97–99, 123–25.

by senators at the hearings were the same as those found in the GAO's audit reports. This coincidence suggests that although some senators may rely directly on the GAO reports, probably the majority receive their information indirectly, through the House, which is in keeping with the Senate's traditional "appellate role" —serving as a forum for review of House Appropriations Committee actions.[18]

In contrast to the minimal direct use of GAO reports in appropriation hearings of the Senate, a review of TVA hearings before the House Subcommittee on Public Works Appropriations (of the Committee on Appropriations) disclosed significant use of these reports on several occasions. A look at two specific hearings on TVA's budget will illustrate how the GAO's findings may be used.[19]

In the second session of the Eighty-fifth Congress, in reviewing TVA's budget request for fiscal year 1959, the Republican side of the subcommittee (Congressmen Ivor D. Fenton, Pennsylvania; Ben F. Jensen, Iowa; and Hamer H. Budge, Idaho) made extensive use of the GAO's findings, referring specifically to the GAO's *Audit Report for Fiscal Year 1957*.

[18] On the question of the House and Senate roles in the appropriations process, see, for example, Aaron Wildavsky, *The Politics of the Budgetary Process* (Boston: Little, Brown and Company, 1964) especially pp. 47–56; and Fenno, *The Power of the Purse,* especially ch. 10. Congressional staff and GAO officials interviewed in the course of this study generally agreed that this picture of the use made of GAO audit reports by the Senate and House appropriations committees is essentially accurate and reflects the usual appropriations roles of the Senate and House appropriations committees. The fact is, the Senate Appropriations Committee would ordinarily not be expected to use the GAO reports to the same extent as does the House committee. For a more general discussion of these differences in the House and Senate, see the excellent, brief discussion in Nelson W. Polsby, "Policy Analysis and Congress," in U.S., Congress, Joint Economic Committee, *The Analysis and Evaluation of Public Expenditures: The PPB System*, 91st Cong., 1st sess., 1969, Joint Committee Print, Vol. III, 944–47.

[19] For purposes of clarification, appropriations hearings for, say fiscal year 1959, would ordinarily be held in the spring of 1958. At that time, congressmen would have before them the GAO audit report of TVA activities for fiscal year 1957.

Mr. Jensen questioned TVA witnesses about the fact "that TVA charged the Federal agencies more for power than it does its industrial and commercial users (page 276 of hearing document)."

Mr. Fenton expressed his concern over TVA's coal procurement policies. He insisted that the relevant part of GAO's audit report be placed in the record (pages 285–92).

Mr. Budge asked the TVA board chairman whether the comptroller general had ruled on TVA's construction of additions to its existing steam plants (pages 299–300). He, too, was concerned about TVA power charges to federal power users, as pointed out by the GAO (pages 308–309 and 346–47).

In the first session of the Eighty-sixth Congress, as the House subcommittee looked at the proposed TVA budget for 1960, the use of the GAO's *Audit Report for Fiscal Year 1958* was more bipartisan in nature.

In responding to questions by Chairman Clarence Cannon (Democrat, Missouri) concerning turbogenerators purchased from Westinghouse, the TVA board chairman referred to GAO's findings on this issue as a part of his explanation (page 872 of hearing document).

Congressman Joe L. Evins (Democrat, Tennessee), discussing TVA's pending bond-financing legislation, asked: "Would the GAO continue to audit all of TVA's operations and file its reports . . . to the Congress?" TVA responded in the affirmative, and Evins concluded: "Of course, this charge that the Congress would lose control is spurious and not in reality true (pages 881–82)."

The Republican side of the subcommittee, however, was still to be heard. Mr. Fenton first questioned the TVA board chairman about the GAO's organizational recommendations relating to TVA's agricultural and chemical program (pages 899–900). Then, Mr. Fenton also wanted to know: "Was the Comptroller General correct when he informed a member of this committee that the TVA . . . issued letters of intent on contracts for a steam plant unit before it transmitted its budget to Congress?" He continued: "Will you give us a yes or no answer whether or not the Comptroller General was correct?" The TVA board chairman replied: "I think he is correct in fact there; yes." TVA later submitted for the record a letter arguing that while the GAO was correct, it had not considered all the facts (pages 900–901).

Well aware of the importance of the appropriations process to all executive agency programs and proposals, the GAO has made a special effort to provide investigative assistance in this area. The efforts apparently have been successful. GAO officials meet periodically with appropriations subcommittee staff members and furnish to the House Appropriations Committee a summary of the most important audit findings each year. Almost 250 references to these findings were made during appropriations hearings in the Eighty-eighth Congress, according to the *1965 Annual Report* of the GAO (page 20). In fact, of the 14 examples of GAO findings with regard to TVA that were described in chapter 3, 7 were later referred to in appropriations hearings alone.

IV

The special hearing, the third main type of hearing that documents Congress's use of GAO audit findings, is a special tool of the House and Senate committees on government operations to investigate any problem or question which seems to merit further attention. The following is an account of one such hearing by the House Committee on Government Operations.

A particularly lively one, this hearing was held on January 25, 1962, by the Subcommittee on Executive and Legislative Reorganization. At issue was the legality of TVA's procedure for making purchases of urgently needed property or services costing less than $5,000, a procedure questioned by the GAO in its audit report for the 1960 fiscal year. It was the GAO's contention that specific legislative authority should be obtained if TVA were to continue this practice. The committee, in commenting on the import of the hearing, noted that:

> The TVA urgent purchase policy was brought to the attention of the Congress by the Comptroller General's report. The committee was of the opinion that a significant question of interpretation of law was raised by the urgent purchase policy. Since the dollar volume of urgent purchases by TVA was comparatively

small, the significance of the question arose from the potential danger of the policy's being mistakenly used as a precedent by less circumspect agencies or later TVA Boards for weakening the competitive process.[20]

Present at the hearing were Congressman William L. Dawson, chairman of both the full committee and the subcommittee, Neal Smith (Democrat, Iowa), Clarence J. Brown (Republican, Ohio), and John B. Anderson (Republican, Illinois). Congressional staff members present included the subcommittee's counsel and investigator and the full committee's general counsel, associate general counsel, and minority counsel. Representing TVA were its board chairman, solicitor, director of purchasing, and Washington representative. The GAO was represented by its assistant general counsel, one of its congressional liaison attorneys, and its auditing supervisory accountant in charge of the TVA audit in question.

The issue dated back to December of 1959 when the TVA Board of Directors approved a policy that permitted urgent purchases to be made without the customary advertising, posting, and public opening of sealed bids. Although the TVA Act of 1933 had exempted certain emergency procurements from the requirements of advertised bidding, the Board's policy had broadened the exemptions to embrace "urgent" (as contrasted with "emergency") TVA needs. Most procurements under the new procedure were being made merely by telephoning two to five suppliers who then furnished oral quotations. The dollar volume of these purchases was not considered significant by the committee, in terms of the total TVA budget, but the sum had reached almost $7.5 million in fiscal year 1961.

To the GAO, the TVA procedure was inconsistent with the TVA Act and, in failing to give reasonable publicity to the proposed purchases, did not give the government the benefit of all available competition. TVA's position was that the TVA Act granted broad discretion in regard to advertising and that, acting within

[20] U.S., Congress, House, Committee on Government Operations, *Tennessee Valley Authority Urgent Purchases*, 87th Cong., 2nd sess., 1962, Rept. 2152, p. 2.

this discretion, the Board merely adopted a less formal method of advertising. The GAO countered with the statement that, if TVA's interpretation were correct, then the Board could at any time raise the amount of a procurement under this policy far higher than $5,000.[21]

The hearing opened in what seemed to be a cordial manner, with Congressman Brown asking the TVA Board chairman to sit across the table from him—"I learned long ago to always look generals in the eye." It developed, however, that Congressman Brown's remark was more than mere banter. First he made it clear he did not like TVA's approach: it "has always been my understanding, that in order to protect the taxpayer, all Federal bids and Federal business must be on the basis of written contracts and written bids, and not just somebody saying over the phone, 'Yes, Charlie, that is fine! and Charlie changes his mind the next day . . . .' " GAO's assistant general counsel, momentarily forgetting why a hearing was being held and whose side he was on, announced that "there have been cases . . . where the receipt and acceptance of oral bids have been sanctioned by the General Accounting Office . . . ." Congressman Brown then decided to teach the GAO as well as the TVA a lesson. He reminded the GAO attorney that the GAO was an arm of Congress and asked:

> What authority do you have to change the written law of this country . . . ? I get a new education every day. I have not been around here very long, only a quarter of a century, but every day I learn something new. Now we have the General Accounting Office making law and interpreting law and approving statutes contrary to law.[22]

When the hearing finally returned to the question of TVA's urgent purchase policy, most of the rest of the discussion centered on the uses of "emergency" as opposed to "urgent" purchases and other questions mainly of a semantic nature. Congressman Brown, growing impatient, concluded:

[21] U.S., Congress, House, Subcommittee of the House Committee on Government Operations, *Hearings, Tennessee Valley Authority Urgent Purchases*, 87th Cong., 2nd sess., 1962, pp. 1–2.

[22] *Ibid.*, pp. 9–10.

Now, let me say this to you. There are a great many of us around here, and we are not so much worried about what men of the caliber of [TVA's board chairman] will do on these things; we have found that most of our troubles come from smart young lawyers that are scattered around; they are finding clever and devious ways to get around the intent and the purpose and acts of Congress.[23]

One of the most interesting if tangential aspects of the hearings was Chairman Dawson's statement on the GAO and its usefulness to the Congress. He warmly endorsed that organization's work saying, "They have saved millions and millions of dollars for the people of this country," and then added that "they are justified in raising this question." He concluded:

I think that the Department [TVA] should get together with the GAO, which represents the Congress. Now, you don't want any trouble with us, and we certainly don't want to make trouble for you. But if the two things come head to head, I have an idea who is going to win. It seems to me as simple as that.[24]

The report of the hearing, under the heading "Action Taken by the Tennessee Valley Authority as a Result of Hearings and Investigation," stated that the committee had been informed, hardly a month after the hearing, that the TVA Board had abandoned its "urgent," nonemergency purchasing policy. The committee then commended the TVA Board for acting promptly to eliminate the objectionable feature from the Authority's rules.

Thus, by a combination of law, tradition, and policy the GAO's service to the U.S. Congress translates in practice into service to any congressional committee desiring such help, whether the concern be government operations, appropriations, or legislative. As far as resources permit, assistance is also given to individual members of Congress. The committees on government operations in the Senate and House, charged officially with receiving the GAO audit reports in Congress, have informally worked out an arrangement for using the GAO and its audit services while at the same time avoiding duplication and overlap. One specific

23 *Ibid.,* p. 20.
24 *Ibid.,* p. 29.

way in which the Congress and its committees use the GAO's audit expertise can be documented readily by reference to hearings held by the committees on government operations, the appropriations committees, and the legislative committees. In the case of TVA the record shows that all three kinds of committees—particularly on the House side—use GAO audit reports and the information they contain in congressional committee hearings. As will be seen, the GAO also provides many other services to Congress.

V. WORKING WITH CONGRESS
AND OTHER AGENCIES

AN important aspect of the GAO's total usefulness to the government is the quality of its relations with Congress and with the agencies it audits. Little progress of a lasting nature could be expected, nor could full potential be realized, in an atmosphere charged with constant bickering, suspicion, distrust, and a mutual lack of confidence. In the examination of this facet of the GAO, the strong and well-established TVA organization once again serves as a model focal point. The relations between this agency and the GAO can be used as a study in microcosm not only to describe GAO tactics and suggest what its experience may be with other agencies, but also to indicate the measure of the GAO's acceptance by Congress now and in the future.

I

In the case of TVA, as has been seen, the agency-to-agency relations have not always been as cordial as they are today. For example, on December 19, 1942, David Lilienthal, then chairman of TVA's Board of Directors, wrote in his *Journals*:

Spent an hour with the Comptroller General. Although he says clearly that he thinks we are doing a "grand job" and that our books are in very good order, he feels he must file with Congress some reports prepared by his predecessor going back to 1934 that are terrible, full of inflammatory general charges that his entire staff agrees are without foundation . . . . If those reports are filed, no matter what the disavowal, it will be terrible—a smear that will give McKellar just the opening he has been looking for.[1]

[1] David E. Lilienthal, *The TVA Years, 1939–1945*, Vol. I of *The Journals of David E. Lilienthal* (New York: Harper and Row, Publishers, 1964), p. 574.

In this brief statement, Mr. Lilienthal indicated the extent of the strain between TVA and GAO in the past and how the GAO findings might be "misused" as well as employed constructively. David Lilienthal was worried, in 1942, about what Senator Kenneth D. McKellar (Democrat, Tennessee) might do with GAO's data, for at that time a bitter Lilienthal-McKellar feud was in progress. Indeed, this problem of the use made of GAO findings is always a matter of concern to the agencies being studied. For instance, when the GAO opposed TVA's power-financing proposal, private power interests and Chamber of Commerce representatives pointed approvingly to the GAO's stand. On the other hand, friends of TVA, such as Senator Lister Hill, apparently ignored the GAO's objections while at the same time pointing to the GAO as the "watchdog" that would maintain congressional control over TVA. And again, critics of the Authority seem to be highly interested in the GAO reports when the time comes for TVA appropriations hearings. In fact, there are few available examples of sincere efforts to evaluate the GAO findings and ask for TVA's comment as the logical prelude to objective action. In addition, TVA critics in Congress are too often content to use GAO's findings without following through to see that some solution to the problem is reached. Even TVA's friends apparently use the GAO findings only when it suits their purpose of the moment. As a result, and through no fault of its own, much of the lasting value of the GAO's work is lost.

In recent years, even though memories of the old days still linger, TVA-GAO cooperation has been excellent. The extent of the cooperation is surprising to those who remember the former bitterness. Harvey Mansfield made a prophetic comment on this point in *The Comptroller General* in 1939:

> To summarize, the Comptroller General's relations with the TVA over the five-year period since 1933 have imposed on the government a direct cost of upwards of $200,000. For this there is precisely nothing to show except damage to morale, interference with the conduct of important operations, and a flood of unjustified public suspicion on the work of honest officials which reaches far beyond the TVA and tends to undermine popular confidence in the capacity of government

enterprise generally . . . . But with the settlement of its internal dissentions, the subsidence of political passions against it, and the cessation of litigation involving its life, together with a smoother routine when its construction program is accomplished, it will no longer be as vulnerable as in the past to the pettier harassments that are the stock in trade of the General Accounting Office. It is unlikely that the Comptroller General will again venture so drastic a step as to threaten a complete interruption of the Authority's activities.[2]

In other words, the GAO's determination not to repeat its early mistakes undoubtedly has aided the GAO-TVA relationship.

The improved relations may also be owing to a more concrete factor, however: the fact that TVA has so often had its way in Congress when differences have arisen with the GAO. As mentioned previously, a 1935 amendment to the TVA Act required that all GAO reports be sent to TVA for review and that TVA's comments be included in the report to Congress. The joint congressional committee investigating TVA in 1939 severely criticized the GAO's methods and competence in auditing TVA. A 1941 amendment to the TVA Act stated that the GAO had no disallowance power over TVA expenditures, and that TVA could determine its own accounting system. The bond-financing amendment to the TVA Act in 1959 was still another legislative victory for the TVA over the GAO. Under this amendment, and contrary to GAO advice, the development of the TVA power system need not depend on congressional appropriations and is, therefore, considerably more independent of congressional control. In addition, TVA is legally freed from the restriction in the Government Corporation Control Act of 1945 that forbids the use of private accounting firms for auditing the records of government corporations. When the amendment was first passed, the GAO made important concessions to convince TVA that it need not employ a private accounting firm. For example, GAO offered the timely issuance of commercial-type, short-form audit reports of TVA's financial statements for use in connection with TVA's bond sales. Later the GAO informed TVA that in making up such reports the GAO

---

[2] Mansfield, *The Comptroller General*, pp. 243–44.

would willingly cooperate with a private auditing firm, but that the private audit was not necessary. In spite of this assurance, TVA has continued to use the private audit, and it plans to do so in the future for three reasons: (1) the private audit is probably essential to TVA's bond sales in the private sector; (2) TVA cannot take the chance of having, in any given year, a GAO report spread confusion or raise questions in bond markets; and (3) TVA considers the private audit very important as a countercheck of the GAO audit and as a means of lessening its importance. The GAO recognizes that it must have a very good case before disagreeing basically, or too often, with an internationally-known private accounting firm. It is true that the private audit is not truly comprehensive (for example, it does not look at management practices as such but only at their results), yet it does exist, and because it does, it must be taken into consideration by the GAO. Thus, new meaning is given to the GAO's statement that "our audit was limited to observations and tests of their [the private firm's] audit work and such other auditing procedures as we considered necessary in the circumstances."[3]

Even the Government Corporation Control Act of 1945 apparently has not made TVA more subservient to the GAO in spite of the view commonly held at the time of its enactment. This view, according to Gerald G. Schulsinger in *The General Accounting Office: Two Glimpses,* held that the new act would essentially end the day of the autonomous public corporation because the GAO either could not or would not develop a comprehensive, commercial-type audit but would rather employ its old techniques to reduce the corporation's fiscal freedom.[4] This view, in the case of TVA at least, has not materialized. On the contrary, the GAO did apply new auditing techniques geared to TVA's corporate status, with the result that TVA has largely preserved its corporate freedom and at the same time improved its relations with the GAO.

A special follow-up procedure employed by the GAO enhances the value of its audit work to TVA. Annually the comptroller

[3] General Accounting Office, *Audit Report of TVA, 1966*, p. 1.
[4] P. 37.

general sends a copy of one of the GAO's congressional reports—"Compilation of General Accounting Office Findings and Recommendations For Improving Government Operations"—to TVA's Board chairman because the report contains useful information on actual and possible improvements in government operations. TVA files indicate that the reports are used to advantage, although still greater use could be made of these reports.

TVA also uses the GAO's reports on other federal agencies that have similar responsibilities to keep abreast of interests and interpretations of both the GAO and Congress. At one TVA Board meeting, GAO reports on the Bonneville Power Administration, the Bureau of Reclamation, the Southeastern Power Administration, and the Southwestern Power Administration were used to check the proposed financing of a TVA power project.[5] Thus, judging by TVA's experience, the work of the GAO is clearly valuable to federal agencies, and most of these agencies could no doubt take fuller advantage of it than they do.[6]

Concerning the use made of the GAO by the executive branch of the government, Charles Hyneman writes:

> The appropriations acts of Congress are enactments of law; being law, they must be obeyed. They are, however, subject to different interpretations . . . . The General Accounting Office shares the task of interpreting the appropriations acts . . . . Officials in the administrative departments and agencies frequently discuss with officials of the General Accounting Office the intent of Congress and the legal effect of appropriation language.[7]

Unquestionably, Congress does not always get all the facts about the particular audit issue it is considering, and this lack impairs its supervisory function. A key question is: To what extent do the GAO and the agency it is working with bargain over the content or the wording of issues that go into the audit reports? Such bargaining could rob the issues of much of their significance

[5] TVA general manager's files, "Nickajack Financing," Jan. 27, 1964.

[6] More detail on this important point can be found in ch. 6, including a discussion of how Secretary of Defense Robert McNamara made use of the GAO audit report in the management of the Department of Defense, and of congressional interest in Secretary McNamara's use of the GAO's work.

[7] Hyneman, *Bureaucracy in a Democracy*, p. 130.

and thus withhold complete knowledge from Congress. Research suggests that this is an ever-present possibility. Concern over this kind of problem prompted political scientist Richard Neustadt to write:

> Bureaucracy has brought a new contestant into play: the great prospective struggle is between entrenched officialdom and politicians everywhere, White House and Hill alike. Officialdom already is competitive with both . . . . It seems far from certain that the bureaucrats will not learn how to close their ranks.[8]

Fortunately this concern is one that Congress has not completely overlooked, as evidenced in a report issued in 1956 by a special study subcommittee of the House Committee on Government Operations:

> The subcommittee believes that the quality and effectiveness of reports issued by the General Accounting Office could be improved.
>
> The annual reports of the Comptroller General have not furnished sufficient information about the adequacy and effectiveness of the accounting of Government agencies, and the manner in which the agencies are carrying out their financial responsibilities.
>
> . . . Reports issued by the General Accounting Office . . . seem to indicate that too much consideration may have been given to revisions of draft reports in response to the views of the agencies before reports are issued and transmitted to the Congress.[9]

It is obvious that the GAO reports, to be of maximum usefulness to Congress, must be complete and objective, unaltered by bureaucratic compromise and committee decision. Conflicting agency views can still be aired, but through the medium of separate reports attached to the GAO documents.

The GAO reports to Congress on TVA have produced various results. One finding led to a special hearing before a subcommittee of the House Committee on Government Operations. In

[8] Richard E. Neustadt, "Politicians and Bureaucrats," in Truman, *The Congress and America's Future*, p. 119.

[9] U.S., Congress, House, Committee on Government Operations, *The General Accounting Office*, pp. 3–4.

the case of TVA's bond-financing legislation, the GAO's advice was at least partly taken in the final action by Congress. A few minor issues were settled within TVA, before reaching Congress at all, sometimes resulting in the GAO's favor and sometimes in a stand-off in which TVA apparently changed certain minor practices but actually retained them in another form. The fact that only a few issues were settled in Congress and that the larger part of the GAO's findings merely provided material for debate, leaving the issues themselves unresolved, indicates the need for still greater congressional follow-through on the GAO reports.

The turbulent early history of GAO-TVA relations may be attributed to the fact that in the beginning a relatively new and controversial agency, the GAO, was called upon to audit the work of an even newer and more controversial agency, the TVA. Neither agency was really certain of its responsibilities, much less of how to perform them. Furthermore, from TVA's point of view, its corporate form of organization was, among other things, an effort to escape from the government-wide administrative rules applied by the comptroller general. Thus, conflict was inevitable, but not entirely without compensation. The vastly improved relations of today are in part derived from the conflicts of the past, which actually defined the roles of the two agencies more precisely and thereby led to more efficient cooperation. Furthermore, these conflicts provided lessons for government-wide application.

In the future, GAO-TVA relations may well depend on GAO's long-range goals. For instance, GAO is presently seeking clarification and settlement of several basic financial issues involving power and resource-development agencies, including TVA, the Bonneville Power Administration, the Bureau of Reclamation, the Corps of Engineers, the Southeastern Power Administration, and the Southwestern Power Administration. In addition, the agency has just begun a complete investigation of TVA's non-power operations.[10]

[10] Interviews with GAO officials; "TVA Non-Power Probe Planned," *Knoxville News Sentinel*, Nov. 22, 1968, and other news clippings from TVA files.

II

Regarding the Budget and Accounting Act of 1921 that created the U.S. General Accounting Office, the chairman of the House committee that handled the bill said:

> It was the intention of the committee that the Comptroller General should be something more than a bookkeeper or accountant; that he should be a real critic; and at all times should come to Congress, no matter what the political complexion of Congress or the Executive might be, and point out inefficiency . . . .[11]

Congressman Martin B. Madden (Republican, Illinois), who was later to become chairman of the House Appropriations Committee, commenting on the same legislation, said:

> If I have my way, when this legislation is completed, I shall propose the creation of a great committee of the House, to be known as the Committee on Expenditures, consisting of the best men in the House because it is to be a great committee . . . to whom this auditor and Comptroller General may report from day to day, and through this medium supply the House of Representatives and the Senate with such information as to what is being done with the money appropriated as to keep the Congress advised in connection with every step taken.[12]

Although the proposed "Committee on Expenditures" as recommended by Congressman Madden did not materialize in exactly the form he envisioned, the present-day committees on government operations have come to serve essentially the same function.

Today, after a lengthy period of poor direction and lost opportunity, the GAO has moved much closer to the ideal relationship envisioned by its sponsors. The increasing use by Congress of GAO reports substantiates this view. As eminent a scholar of the legislative process as George Galloway reported that with

[11] General Accounting Office, *Annual Report, 1962*, p. 17.
[12] U.S., Congress, House, Committee on Government Operations, *Notes on the Jurisdiction of the House Committee on Government Operations,* 86th Cong., 1st sess., 1959, p. 3.

the passage of the Legislative Reorganization Act of 1946, " . . . Congress is now so organized as to give full attention to the GAO reports and to obtain action on them. Encouraged by this provision, the General Accounting Office has expanded its reporting function in recent years."[13] The Eightieth Congress (1947–48) received 56 audit reports from the GAO, while in fiscal year 1969 alone the first session of the ninety-first Congress, its committees, and members received 381 audit reports. And these figures do not include an even greater growth in the number of reports made to departments and agencies.[14] As early as 1949, a report of the House Committee on Expenditures in the Executive Departments (later renamed the Committee on Government Operations) stated:

> One of the most far-reaching and telling functions of the General Accounting Office is that of reporting. The function places at the command of the Congress a facility for close scrutiny of the conduct of the financial business of the Government . . . . That the Congress and the agencies are becoming more and more aware of the value of the reports of the Comptroller General is reflected in the tremendously increased number of requests in recent years for reports to be made. In addition to the reports required by law and those specifically requested, the Comptroller General has made hundreds of voluntary reports.[15]

In his *Professional Staffs of Congress,* Kenneth Kofmehl comments:

> For the most part congressional response to the GAO's expanded role has been favorable. Committee hearings, committee reports, the *Congressional Record,* newspapers, and periodicals have been filled with praise for help received from the GAO by members and committees of Congress.[16]

[13] George B. Galloway, *The Legislative Process in Congress* (New York: Thomas Y. Crowell Company, 1955), p. 115.

[14] Information taken from U.S., Congress, Senate, Committee on Government Operations, *Financial Management*, p. 122, and General Accounting Office, *Annual Report, 1969*, p. 4.

[15] U.S., Congress, House, Committee on Expenditures in the Executive Departments, *The General Accounting Office*, p. 27.

[16] P. 227.

Ample evidence to support Kofmehl's appraisal may be found in the annual reports of the GAO, which not only present the GAO's view of its service but also contain the remarks of members of Congress. For example, in its *Annual Report for Fiscal Year 1957* the GAO announced (page 9) that an Office of Legislative Liaison was established to bring about an even closer relationship with Congress. The office was designed to help the GAO keep in daily contact with the committees and with individual members of Congress. The same report discussed the activities report of the House Committee on Government Operations, which commented on a series of developments, including rearrangement of the committee's work program to handle better the GAO's audit reports and the commencement of weekly meetings between the committee and GAO staff members to discuss the reports.

Similarly, *The Annual Report of the Comptroller General for Fiscal Year 1959* (page 22) declares: "In a report to the Congress detailing its activities the House Committee [on Government Operations] noted expressly its good working relationship with our Office as contemplated by the Legislative Reorganization Act of 1946." The *1960 Annual Report* (pages 15–16) states with understandable pride: "The majority leader of the House of Representatives . . . said [on the floor of the House]: 'I have found the General Accounting Office to be objective, factual, and always in the public interest.' "

The *Annual Report for Fiscal Year 1961* contains statements of praise (page 48) for the GAO by the chairman of both the House and Senate committees on government operations. The *Annual Report for Fiscal Year 1964* (page 20) quotes from a report of the Senate Appropriations Committee:

> The committee believes that there has been a lack of prompt and adequate attention given by the agencies to recommendations contained in reports of the General Accounting Office . . . . The committee shares the views of the President of the United States in his remarks to the press, on May 2, 1964, following a Cabinet meeting in which he outlined a nine-point program to achieve greater efficiency and economy in Government operations. Included in the program was his request that

"all reports made by the General Accounting Office and congressional committees be given prompt and thorough and careful attention."

Comments of this nature, which permeate recent annual reports of the GAO, indicate that the GAO-Congress relationship is a close one, and that Congress is well aware of the GAO's contribution and is attaching greater importance to it. The reports also show the increasing esteem in which the GAO is held by the executive branch. This impression was strengthened as a result of a number of interviews with agency and GAO officials and with congressional staff members in Washington.[17]

Certainly as significant as the informal comments and reactions obtained in interviews, and the praise contained in GAO annual reports, are the views of Congress as expressed in congressional reports and documents. In a 1956 document, for example, the Senate Committee on Government Operations complimented the GAO for extending the lessons gained from the commercial-type or comprehensive audits (required by the Government Corporation Control Act of 1945) to the noncorporate agencies "as a means for fuller and more effective discharge of the Comptroller General's responsibility to the Congress." The committee saw great value in the GAO audit reports both to government agencies and to Congress, including the appropriations and legislative committees.[18] A House report similarly noted with approval the GAO's shift in emphasis from the concept of settling accounts to a new concept of auditing executive agencies and reporting the results to Congress. The report also made suggestions for further improving GAO's usefulness to Congress.[19]

The annual appropriation hearing, when the proposed budget of an agency is considered, is perhaps the best indicator of the quality of that agency's relationship with Congress. In the case of the GAO, the indicators have pointed to a good relationship. In recent years the GAO's appropriations hearings have been car-

[17] A list of these interviews is included in the bibliography.

[18] U.S., Congress, Senate, Committee on Government Operations, *Review of Audit Reports*, pp. 4, 26.

[19] U.S., Congress, House, Committee on Government Operations, *The General Accounting Office*, p. 4.

ried out in an atmosphere of rare cordiality. Modest adjustments by the House appropriations subcommittee have been generally accepted by the GAO without appeal to the Senate, although the Senate subcommittee has usually restored, at least in part, even these minor budget reductions made by the House. As might be expected, most House hearings have been far more thorough than those in the Senate.[20]

The results of the GAO's budget hearings in two cases, unusual because of the congressional opposition encountered, offer some additional insights into GAO-congressional relations. At a 1958 hearing the House Subcommittee on Independent Offices imposed a restriction on GAO travel and reduced the budget by $200,000; but the Senate restored $100,000 and the GAO later received a supplemental appropriation of $250,000. At a 1959 House appropriations subcommittee hearing, Congressman Albert Thomas (Democrat, Texas), chairman of the subcommittee, convinced his colleagues that the GAO's proposed budget should be reduced by $350,000. The action had followed Mr. Thomas's objection to the GAO's request for funds to install in government agencies the accrued-expenditure basis for requesting appropriations (as recommended in the second Hoover Commission report). As a member also of the Defense Appropriations Subcommittee, Mr. Thomas had feared that such a system would weaken Congress's control over agency expenditures. Far from endorsing the subcommittee's cut, however, the full Congress not only restored the $350,000 but also awarded the GAO $750,000 over its budget request.

More typical of recent GAO budget hearings, however, was Mr. Thomas's statement in 1960 when he referred to the GAO as " . . . our own GAO . . . . It is the agency of the Congress. The eyes and ears and sometimes . . . the brains" (page 1035). In the 1962 appropriations hearings, Senator Warren G. Magnuson (Democrat, Washington), chairman of the Senate Subcommittee on Independent Offices, stated: " . . . I have often thought there

[20] See ch. 4 for a discussion of the House and Senate roles in the appropriations and audit processes.

was too much limitation on your travel allowance in the past, but I see the House has it up $250,000. Is that sufficient for you?" Told by Comptroller General Campbell that the amount was adequate, the senator continued: " . . . But you have to do a great deal of traveling, with the missions that are assigned to you. I was just wondering if that was enough." He concluded: " . . . I agree with the House when they say the committee thinks the Comptroller General is doing an outstanding job" (pages 307–308). In the 1963 hearing in the House, Congressman Harold C. Ostertag (Republican, New York), stated:

> I want to pay tribute to the job that you and your organization are doing . . . . Within the past few months . . . I have received about twenty of your reports, most of them relating to the Department of Defense. I estimate on the basis of recent reports that you have achieved an actual saving to the Government of about a quarter of a million dollars [page 31].

Ostertag had made similar statements on many other occasions. In September, 1969, the House subcommittee reviewing the GAO's budget request for fiscal year 1970 recommended $63 million for the GAO, only $184,000 below the agency's request, and this amount in a tight budget period for the federal government as a whole. The Senate subcommittee reported the same amount, and the Congress appropriated the $63 million for fiscal year 1970. Such an unending flow of praise and good fortune, often bipartisan in nature, would sound strange to most other departments and agencies of the federal government.

The good relations between the GAO and these committees apparently is on a realistic rather than a sentimental basis, however. Some penetrating questions are asked, and the GAO is expected to answer them satisfactorily. For example, at the 1963 House appropriations subcommittee hearings, Congressman Charles R. Jonas (Republican, North Carolina) asked about the growth of the GAO budget from about $32 million in fiscal 1953 to nearly $44 million for fiscal 1963, especially in view of the decrease in GAO personnel during that period. In reply, the comptroller general mentioned a change in quality and composition of

GAO's work force, additional employee benefits, increased emphasis on travel, and the general rise in the cost of living (page 32). The House subcommittee report on the fiscal year 1970 appropriations demonstrated that the Congress keeps a close eye on new developments and directions within the GAO. This document raised some pointed questions about the GAO's involvement in current policy problem matters and in the program-planning-budgeting fields.[21]

Still another, quite recent, hearing further demonstrates that the GAO cannot depend on sentimentality or on its past achievements to maintain congressional support. At a hearing of the Joint Economic Committee to investigate defense procurement, Senator William Proxmire (Democrat, Wisconsin) angrily criticized defense contractors and Defense Department officials for refusing to appear before his committee and testify. He and his colleagues also criticized Comptroller General Elmer Staats for not pushing the GAO's recommendations more vigorously on how to monitor DOD spending. Proxmire added: "We would like to call you our 'watchdog.' But on the basis of your response to this committee, we wonder if we should . . . the GAO makes excuses and excuses. I don't know where we can turn."[22]

In the final analysis, however, the Congress looks upon the GAO, one of its chief sources of staff assistance, in a most favorable light. Even Joseph Harris, one of the GAO's sternest critics, concedes this point:

> Records of congressional hearings participated in by representatives of the GAO, especially when the Comptroller General

[21] All information taken from hearings and reports of the House and Senate appropriations subcommittees for fiscal years 1957–70, specific references as cited in text, as follows: The GAO appeared before the appropriations subcommittees on independent offices in connection with the appropriations requests for fiscal years 1957–64. For fiscal year 1965, GAO budget hearings were before the subcommittees on legislative branch appropriations, and for the following two years hearings were again before the subcommittees on independent offices. Appropriations hearings for fiscal years since 1968 have been before the legislative branch subcommittees.

[22] Warren Unna, "Arms Firms Assailed by Proxmire," *Washington Post,* June 14, 1969.

himself appears, abound with expressions of mutual appreciation. On Capitol Hill, the Comptroller General is accorded a
deference comparable to that given the Director of the FBI.[23]

This attitude is fundamental to greater future involvement by
the GAO in providing needed assistance to the Congress.

[23] Harris, *Congressional Control,* p. 160.

VI. AIDING THE CONGRESS

O NE way of measuring and testing the value of the work of any organization is to compare its activities and accomplishments against some sort of initial "job description." Fortunately, in the case of the GAO a good beginning set of standards is already available. Joseph Harris has established several key criteria which, in his opinion, must be met before the GAO, through its audit system, can realize its full potential as an aid to the United States Congress in its control of administrative performance:

1. The GAO must be independent of the executive branch and responsible only to Congress.

2. The GAO audit must be a true post-audit.

3. The audit must be comprehensive, intensive, and promptly executed.

4. Congress must be organized to receive, consider, and act on audit reports.[1]

And in addition to Mr. Harris's standards, it is suggested here that two others should be added to the list:

5. The GAO must be professionally competent and as objective as possible in a political environment—that is, not politically motivated.

6. The results of the GAO's audit work must be significant, and the audit effort must deal with a variety of timely issues that are important to Congress and to the departments and agencies directly concerned.

How, then, does the GAO fare when measured against these standards? The conclusion suggested by this study is that the

[1] Harris, *Congressional Control*, pp. 140–41.

agency comes quite close to meeting the indicated requirements, with the possible exception of criterion four as described above.

1. In regard to the first criterion, there is little doubt, in law and in fact, that the GAO clearly recognizes that it exists solely to serve Congress, and that Congress regards the GAO as a useful extension of its staff. To be sure, the GAO has definite ideas about its own role and how best to fulfill that role, but to date these ideas seem generally to have conformed to, rather than conflicted with, its role as seen by Congress. If the need should arise, Congress can always exert further control through the all-powerful appropriations process.

2. The GAO does well also in meeting the requirement that its audit be a true post-audit. No longer does the GAO ask to approve agency disbursements in advance. In fact, it gives advice on proposed disbursements only when so requested by agency accounting officers. It is true that agency transactions still do not become final until the comptroller general has approved them by settling the agency's accounts, but this function is hardly a pre-audit in the traditional sense. Today the GAO settles an agency's accounts by testing transactions for legality, on a sampling basis, as a part of the GAO's post-audit work. To be precise, it is a pre-settlement audit, or check, but a post-payment audit. And disallowance of agency expenditures as a part of the settlement of accounts is becoming less and less significant as a part of the GAO's changing audit approach.

The increased reliance of the GAO on comprehensive, commercial-type audit procedures—an outgrowth of the Government Corporation Control Act—and the GAO's cooperative ventures with the executive branch in joint-accounting and financial-management undertakings have eliminated, to a great extent, the relevancy and accuracy of the charge of pre-audit, although the charge is still made by many, including Mr. Harris, whose criteria are being used here. Perhaps the GAO's changing view of its power to settle agency accounts and disallow expenditures means that this GAO activity is no longer as detrimental to executive responsibility on the one hand, and true congressional supervision on the other, as is so commonly asserted in traditional public-administration theory. Indeed, it can be argued that a post-payment settlement of accounts is a fundamental part of a post-audit. It is possible that traditional theory on this point has not only failed to keep pace with recent developments, but has also been based on false premises in many respects.

It should again be noted in this connection that TVA and other government corporations (unlike other agencies that the GAO audits) are not subject to the disallowance power of the GAO. The 1941 amendment to the TVA Act clarified this issue by stating that the TVA Board and not the comptroller general was the authoritative and final interpreter of the statutes dealing with TVA's power to make expenditures. The Government Corporation Control Act did not alter this amendment and did not give the GAO disallowance power over government corporations generally. GAO-TVA working techniques and relations have already been discussed. Whatever shortcomings may exist in other areas, the test of a true post-audit seems to be met in the case of TVA and other government corporations. Perhaps this experience will be transferred more and more to the GAO's dealings with all government agencies and serve to improve further the nature of the GAO's audit activities.[2]

3. Are the audits of the GAO comprehensive, intensive, and promptly executed? The first two parts of the question must be answered in the affirmative. Audits appear to be quite thorough, as well as comprehensive, in scope; and commendable follow-up action is taken by the GAO from year to year.[3] Although the report itself of any single year may not be comprehensive in the usual sense (a common criticism of the GAO), the audit process and

[2] The TVA Act also gives TVA the power to "determine its own system of administrative accounts (sec. 9[b], TVA Handbook)." The joint financial-improvement program of the GAO, Bureau of the Budget, Treasury Department, and Civil Service Commission, discussed earlier, seems to be making substantial progress toward also providing the regular departments and agencies with great flexibility in designing their accounting systems. Accounting systems developed by federal agencies, of course, must meet the broad standards prescribed by the GAO.

[3] See, for example, the GAO's *Annual Report, 1966* and *1967*, which contain a "Restatement of Prior Year Recommendations," pp. 28–30, 34–36, respectively.

procedures upon which the report is based do qualify as comprehensive if viewed over a span of several years. As to follow-up, some agencies regard GAO persistence on a given issue as harassment, but GAO might legitimately complain that some agencies give only lip service to compliance with its recommendations, changing words but not policies, or policies but not practices. A significant factor that influences GAO follow-through on a given issue is the interest shown by Congress in the issue. The agency makes a special effort initially to include in its audit those subjects that seem to be of particular concern to Congress.[4] If Congress fails to help the GAO settle an issue—by means of an investigation, the use of the appropriations process, or some other device—the GAO usually can do no more. Yet there are exceptions. If the issue is significant enough in the view of the GAO, repeated efforts may be made to obtain congressional action. Thus, in the case of the power-rate controversy involving TVA and the Southeastern Power Administration discussed earlier, the GAO eventually recommended to Congress the passage of corrective legislation. The GAO plans to continue to push this legislation.

With regard to the promptness of making audit reports, the evidence is less favorable to the GAO—if one considers service to the audited agencies as well as service to Congress. The audits are available for spring appropriations hearings and are usually submitted in time for most congressional uses. However, they do not always meet, as in TVA's case, the agencies' statutory deadlines for submission of such reports to Congress. Moreover, the reports are often too late for most of the Authority's internal purposes. There is some evidence, too, that the GAO's audits of noncorporate agencies are not made as promptly as those of government corporations. Some agencies claim that the issues discussed in GAO reports have been "taken care of long ago." It should be remembered, however, that the GAO's first responsibility is to Congress; the comptroller general has no legal charge whatsoever to meet the timetable of any particular department or

---

[4] General Accounting Office, *Annual Report, 1966*, p. 8.

agency. Nevertheless, the desirability of efficiency in government suggests that the audit reports should be utilized to the fullest extent possible, and this means that the reports must be made available in time to be helpful to the departments and agencies involved, as well as to Congress. How much weight should be given to these agency complaints about the timing of the reports is not known, but the GAO is now attempting to improve its service in this area.[5]

4. On the question of congressional organization and response to GAO's reports, Joseph Harris flatly states:

> . . . Congress is not adequately organized to receive, consider, and act on the audit reports. The two Committees on Government Operations are the most important in this respect, but the GAO also has close relations with the Appropriations Committees, and from time to time with various subject-matter committees as well. . . . There is no single point of responsibility in either house for supervising the Comptroller General's work and systematically following up on his reports.[6]

Perhaps this criticism is the most telling one of all those that are leveled against the GAO. It is, of course, directed more at Congress than at the GAO, even though the GAO's effectiveness must certainly be judged by how well its work is received, used, and supervised.

Granting that the GAO has many bosses and a fuzzy line of supervision from Congress, one wonders if Congress would be better served by a single joint committee, as will be discussed later, through which all GAO reports would be channeled and to

[5] Internal GAO memorandum from the comptroller general to the heads of all GAO divisions and offices, "Preparation and Processing of Audit Reports," May 3, 1968. The memorandum closed with this message: "In view of my concern [over timely reporting to the Congress and agencies], I am directing that copies of this memorandum be distributed to all staff members involved in accounting and auditing activities. I would hope that it will serve to emphasize that timeliness, as well as quality, is an important factor in the reporting function, and to inculcate a sense of urgency in all of our work in order to eliminate unnecessary delays. At the same time, I realize that, as auditors, we have to make sure that we do not short-cut any necessary procedure to assure ourselves that the information we communicate to the Congress and agencies is reliable."

[6] Harris, *Congressional Control,* p. 159.

which any other committee or congressman would be forced to turn before obtaining the GAO assistance needed. As a matter of practical politics, could this be made to work in the U.S. Congress, given its traditions and present dispersed organization and method of doing business? As for a single point of responsibility in Congress for supervising the GAO's work, Mr. Harris is correct. There is none. A student of administration, uninitiated to the far-reaching interests and probings of the various committees and individual congressmen, would say that the present system cannot work. And it is true that if the GAO's powers and responsibilities are expanded much beyond their present scope, attention must certainly be given to this congressional decentralization. In practice, however, the arrangement at present defies more than it confirms good administrative theory.[7]

The truth is that, despite the absence of a clear-cut chain of command, the system currently is working exceptionally well. The House Committee on Government Operations serves as the GAO's primary link with Congress. This committee receives, reviews, and takes whatever action deemed necessary on the great majority of the GAO reports, which may entail passing some reports on to other interested committees. Its counterpart in the Senate, through an arrangement that minimizes duplication of work by the two committees and apparently is mutually satisfactory, pays far less attention than does the House committee to the routine GAO reports. The Senate committee is generally interested only in the more critical issues—that is, in those reports that reflect a possible violation of law or an improper use of federal funds or property. In addition, the Senate committee calls upon the GAO for a substantial amount of temporary staff assistance to help it with its investigative activities. And on occasion the two committees join together in a cooperative venture to minimize still further duplication, as in 1965 when the committees held joint hearings on the accomplishments and future

---

[7] For some penetrating comments on how the Congress carries out its responsibilities quite successfully, despite what appears to the business-minded as a hopeless, mechanistic set-up, see Polsby, "Policy Analysis," p. 952; Wildavsky, *The Politics of the Budgetary Process*, especially ch. 5.

of the Advisory Commission on Intergovernmental Relations.[8]

When the appropriations or legislative committees ask for special reports from the GAO, informational copies generally go to the House Committee on Government Operations, but these particular reports do not channel through the latter committee, as might be recommended by an administrative specialist. Yet here again, the loosely-structured system seems to work.

In addition to the importance of the GAO's views in legislative committee hearings, previously noted, the agency's work is used in the appropriations process to an extent that is surprising. On page 20 of *GAO Annual Report, 1965,* one finds:

> The Appropriations Committees have for a long time relied on our reports in their consideration of budget requests and each year, by closer liaison, we are able to channel more of our productive effort toward areas of particular concern to the committees and thereby provide them with more timely information and recommendations. For 11 years now we have, at the chairman's request, provided the House Appropriations Committee annually with a composite report of our more significant audit findings compiled under agency headings for easy use during the committee's hearings.

Further, in the GAO reports for 1966 and 1967, there are references to annual meetings between GAO and the staffs of the several appropriations subcommittees to pinpoint areas that the subcommittees thought needed further exploration. Meetings are held after, as well as before, budget hearings to alert the GAO to questions that will require further study before the next hearings are held.

It is true that GAO findings are too often used in appropriations hearings by congressmen who are either opponents or advocates of particular agencies. On the other hand, any use of the audit reports might be termed beneficial in that the problems outlined by the GAO are aired, and GAO officials are given a chance to state

---

[8] U.S., Congress, Subcommittees on Intergovernmental Relations, Senate and House committees on government operations, *Joint Hearings, Five Year Record of the Advisory Commission on Intergovernmental Relations and Its Future Role*, 89th Cong., 1st sess., 1965.

their case. After all, Congress is, among other things, a political organization; the GAO findings will at times, and perhaps often, be used for political reasons. What is needed is enough objective analysis and fact-searching by Congress to neutralize, at least partially, this biased use. One danger of too much political use is that the relations of the GAO with the agencies it audits can be jeopardized by their reaction to the one-sided headlines emanating from Congress. With this fact in mind, it may be in the best interest of both the GAO and the Congress to reach an understanding whereby the GAO, in its audit and investigatory activities, would serve committees but not individual congressmen.

On the whole, the results of congressional follow-through, or corrective action taken, on GAO findings and recommendations have been mixed. On the positive side, there is the example of the late 1950s and early 1960s when the GAO reported on several occasions that it had found in the defense procurement program many instances of overpricing in contracts, caused by inflated or otherwise erroneous estimates of costs by the contracting firms. To rectify this situation, the GAO urged, and even helped draft, corrective legislation that finally became law on September 10, 1962: the Truth-In-Negotiations Act. To cite another case showing positive results, in January, 1968, the GAO concluded a survey for the Joint Economic Committee that showed how federal agencies use discounting procedures and interest-rate policy in evaluating future programs. As a follow-up to this survey, the Joint Economic Committee held hearings in the summer of 1968 on, among other things, a proposed new discount rate for use in the formulation and evaluation of water projects. In fact, this discount rate is now in the process of being raised, a change that is challenging the feasibility of many water projects. This change, therefore, has far-reaching implications for all water agencies, including TVA. In this case as in many others, however, very few people, even in the agencies most directly concerned, are aware of the importance of the GAO's role.[9]

[9] U.S., Congress, Joint Economic Committee, *Hearings, Interest Rate Guidelines for Federal Decision-Making*, 90th Cong., 2nd sess., 1968; in-

The GAO might wish to argue, especially when frustrated by Congress's failure to act on a GAO recommendation, that this lack of follow-through represents the greatest flaw in its service. Yet a congressman, particularly if disagreeing with a certain recommendation, might respond that the GAO has discharged its responsibility when it reports an irregularity to Congress and recommends a corrective measure; whether action is taken is a matter for Congress to decide. Certainly on some occasions congressional failure to act on a GAO recommendation simply indicates disagreement or a lack of enthusiasm for a particular issue. The problem depends in large measure on one's view of GAO-congressional operations, and it must be clear by now that I believe that Congress should listen more often and more carefully to the agency that was created to give it professionally competent advice. If such a premise is accepted, then the present work of the GAO is less than completely successful in terms of results achieved (but not necessarily in terms of its own mandate).

5. Turning to the professional competence and objectivity of GAO personnel, there is little evidence to support the view of some critics that these qualities are lacking. Reports as well as personnel appeared to be refreshingly free of political orientation. The GAO has recently extended its personnel-recruiting efforts to include economists, engineers, and specialists in industrial management and public administration, as well as experts in other disciplines. Also instituted is a systematic program to train the professional staff in advanced data-processing methods and techniques, operations research, and systems analysis and development concepts. Where specific skills are needed and are not available in the GAO, outside consultants are used over short periods. In recent years the GAO has seemed, in the case of TVA, to have a clear understanding of the audited agency and its work. Findings have been clearly stated and, when disagreements have

---

cludes the report by the comptroller general, *Survey of Use by Federal Agencies of the Discounting Technique in Evaluating Future Programs.* A brief description of the GAO's systems-analysis work is contained in General Accounting Office, *Annual Report, 1968,* pp. 57–58.

occurred, TVA has been given ample opportunity to state its views in the audit report, in letters to Congress, and in hearings.

Some critics felt that the GAO was venturing beyond its proper field of interest and competence when it opposed TVA's bond-financing program. Others considered it wrong for the GAO to enter the arena of the public versus private power fight. Some of this criticism arose from inadequate information about the issues, but more of it stemmed from a misunderstanding of the GAO's function. TVA maintained that the bond-financing was needed, first, to prevent future political battles like the one that occurred in the Eisenhower years; and, second, to permit TVA to make long-range plans to serve its residential, commercial, and industrial power customers. The GAO, on the other hand, maintained that if TVA were able to obtain financing from sources other than appropriations, congressional control and supervision would be diminished. The extensive size and independent character of the TVA power operation of today lends weight to the GAO's position, especially when one considers that TVA need do no more than make an annual report (not a request) to Congress on the conduct of its power program, including substantial construction activity.

With the passage of the 1959 bond-financing legislation, the issue was resolved and TVA was no longer required to ask for appropriated funds for its power activities. In 1968, TVA actually spent about $455 million to operate, maintain, and enlarge its power program. All of these funds came from revenues and bond sales—sources independent of Congress. The congressional appropriations that year for the other TVA programs amounted to only about $58 million.[10] This lack of TVA dependence on Congress for the bulk of its funds clearly represents a radical departure from the concept of congressional control and it is not only natural but imperative that the GAO, a congressional agency, be concerned.

Whatever the GAO's point of view on a given issue, Congress has a legitimate right as well as a need to hear it. There are oc-

[10] Tennessee Valley Authority, *Budget Program, 1970*, beginning summary statements.

casional charges, even by congressmen, that the GAO needlessly gets into political controversies, but this view overlooks the true nature of most important government business and tries to separate artificially the administrative from the political. Certainly the issue of bond-financing versus appropriations was a controversial one and also one with political implications; nevertheless, the research for this book has not disclosed a single example of a political decision by the GAO. Indeed, common sense would indicate that the GAO simply cannot afford to let political considerations distort its view of the facts. To do so would be to limit its usefulness to Congress and, therefore, to jeopardize its own future.

This situation does not mean that GAO personnel operate in a vacuum. The GAO is political in the sense that it is very much aware of its environment. Thus, one GAO official, in an interview, fell to discussing the "living politics" of the GAO's work. This official saw the Federal Power Commission's "backing down" on the power-rate issue, first disapproving and then approving the rates at which the Department of the Interior sold power to TVA, as another example of "the hazards of the trade." Another GAO official was found conscientiously reading an article on a forthcoming congressional election. He said, not without a certain wry humor, that he was always interested in staying informed about the trials, tribulations, and makeup of his bosses.

6. Even with a high score on the five other criteria just discussed, the GAO still might not merit its existence unless its findings could be termed significant to Congress and to the executive departments and agencies. This broader question breaks down into two more manageable parts: Does the GAO point to problems on which corrective action should be taken? Does Congress have access from any other sources to the kind of information the GAO supplies?

The record of the GAO's work suggests an emphatic yes to the first question and no to the second, both answers indicating the GAO's significance. Regarding the GAO's attention to problems needing corrective action, its work in the Department of Defense may be cited. Because of the comptroller general's practice of assigning his limited staff to agencies where the big money is spent, about 50 percent of his auditors are assigned to the DOD. In a 1961 hearing, Congressman George Mahon (Democrat, Texas), chairman of the House Subcommittee on Department of Defense Appropriations, asked Robert McNamara, then the relatively new defense secretary, whether the GAO was an aid in managing his department. McNamara said that he met frequently with the comptroller general to ensure close liaison, and added: "I think much more can be done with the General Accounting Office's reports than has been done in the past. I think we can learn about our weaknesses from them."

Again, in a 1963 hearing, Senator Paul Douglas (Democrat, Illinois), chairman of a subcommittee of the Joint Economic Committee, asked McNamara whether his staff had examined a number of GAO reports on the DOD. McNamara replied:

> I can assure you that these reports . . . receive top-level attention. . . . I examine all GAO reports . . . and all of the written replies are reviewed and initialed by either Mr. Gilpatric or me. . . . Many of the actions taken to improve our efficiency can be traced directly to the reports from that office which have come to my personal attention.

Douglas asked the same question again at a 1964 hearing, and McNamara said that every audit report bearing on DOD activity was reviewed by his assistant secretary and comptroller, Mr. Charles J. Hitch, and that a written reply was approved either by the secretary or by his deputy secretary, Mr. Cyrus R. Vance. McNamara added that the reports were usually accurate, and that he had found them to be valuable in bringing deficiencies in the department to his attention[11]

[11] Discussion on the GAO and its audit reports of the activities of the Department of Defense taken, in order, from: U.S., Congress, House, Subcommittee on Department of Defense Appropriations, Committee on Appropriations, *Hearings on the Department of Defense Appropriations (1962)*, 87th Cong., 1st sess., 1961, pp. 62–64; Subcommittee on Defense Procurement, Joint Economic Committee, *Hearings, Impact of Military and Related Civilian Supply and Service Activities on the Economy*, 88th Cong., 1st sess., 1963, p. 35; and same subcommittee and committee, *Hearings, Impact of Military and Related Civilian Supply and Service Activities on the Economy*, 88th Cong., 2nd sess., 1964, pp. 10–11.

Such testimony, especially when it is added to the evidence already presented on GAO-TVA activities, suggests that the GAO is a significant informational and management tool for both executive agencies and Congress. It does indeed point to problems that call for corrective action.

Other tests of significance are also available. For example, if dollar amounts are considered important, many of the GAO's audit findings must be termed significant. In the 1964 Department of Defense hearing cited above, Secretary McNamara stated that the GAO reports directly and indirectly influenced the DOD to increase its volume of competitively-placed contracts by about $900 million a year. The government savings thus effected were not specified, but it may be assumed that shifting a $900-million purchasing operation from a noncompetitive to a competitive basis would involve high stakes. In the TVA's coal-buying operation cited earlier, the amount involved was close to $100 million a year.

Aside from dollar amounts, significance may also be judged by the critical comments or the value judgements contained in the GAO's reports. For example, TVA's urgent-purchases policy (chapters 3 and 4) involved only several million dollars a year and represented only 6 percent to 7 percent of TVA's total purchase of manufactured items. Yet that policy, and the GAO's opinion of it, were important enough to arouse the concern of the House Committee on Government Operations regarding the long-term implications of TVA's novel purchasing procedure, and a hearing was held on the issue. Similarly, evidence of the GAO's influence in clarifying issues—especially issues with important policy content or political overtones—can be found in the role it played in TVA's power-financing legislation for one example, and in the Dixon-Yates controversy for another.

A final question persists: Does Congress have access to this kind of information from any other source? A brief look at some newspaper items involving the GAO and the variety and volume of work it performs for the Congress might help in considering this question. In recent months, defense spending has come under rather careful scrutiny. The GAO reported, for example, that the U.S. Army wasted millions of dollars by rushing ahead with a $1.3 billion Sheridan armored-vehicle program, even though suitable ammunition for the tank's 152-mm guns had never been developed. As a result, more than half of the tanks remained in storage, and the remainder were of limited use. Perhaps more important, an attempt was made to use a "secret" stamp to keep the files on the error closed to auditors and others. The GAO also reported in this period that three of the nation's major defense contractors misused over $18 million of defense funds by financing research and development projects with money earmarked for Minuteman-missile procurement.

The development program for the huge C5A military jet transport held the nation's attention in the news for several weeks. The GAO was not instrumental in identifying this problem, but did eventually perform much of the investigation for Congress on this case, and discovered that Lockheed Aircraft Corporation's project was resulting in total costs of about $1.2 billion above the 1965 estimate of $3.1 billion for the first C5A aircrafts, a 39 percent increase. Finally, in late fall, 1969, the Pentagon announced that it was abandoning its plan to purchase additional C5A cargo transports. The GAO also participated in the investigation of a 1967 military-fuel scandal in Thailand, in which $21 million and at least 5.5 million gallons in fuel and fuel products could not be accounted for. A GAO study disclosed that the fuel in question involved the supply for bases from which U.S. Air Force planes fly combat missions over Vietnam. In one 10-month period alone, 52 percent of all gasoline stored in Thai fuel stations for distribution to U.S. military vehicles was stolen. Bribery, collusion, and government laxity were all involved.

The GAO has also been very active in assisting the Senate Committee on Government Operations in gathering highly technical data in the committee's seven-year-old battle with the Pentagon on the controversial and troubled F111 (TFX) fighter plane. Some versions of the plane have been cancelled and others have been grounded because of structural failures and repeated crashes. The issue here was not so much budgetary overruns or costs, but rather the initial decision-making mechanism in the Pentagon which, in the early 1960s, resulted in former Defense Secretary Robert S. McNamara's reversing the unanimous advice of the military.

Nondefense newspaper accounts involving GAO assistance to the Congress varied widely and included studies of and information on deficiencies in the Medicare, pollution, and anti-poverty programs. On one occasion, hearings were called by a congressional subcommittee to follow up a report in which the GAO disclosed serious deficiencies by the Agricultural Research Service in enforcing insecticide, fungicide, and rodenticide laws.[12]

Major sources of congressional information are the reports of the executive departments and agencies, of course, but they are inevitably documents of self-justification. This is in the nature of both man and organization. Administrators prefer to work in secrecy while Congress, hard-pressed to learn the facts, is in large measure held responsible for administrative acts about which it knows little. For example, Senator Stuart Symington (Democrat, Missouri) was quoted recently in *The Washington Post* (June 2, 1970) charging that the Pentagon denies information to the public, the Congress, and the GAO. By denying the GAO access to documents and other information, congressional oversight is seriously undermined. Interviews conducted during the

---

[12] These newspaper items are merely illustrative of those appearing in recent months. See, for example: "Army Accused of Rushing Work on Tanks to Avoid Budget Study," *New York Times*, May 15, 1969; "GAO Charges Misuse of Minuteman Fund," *Washington Star*, May 10, 1969; "U.S. Scraps Plan to Buy More C-5A's," *Washington Post*, Nov. 15, 1969; "McNamara Concept and 'Total Package' Puts C5A Costs Sky-High," *Washington Daily News,* June 3, 1969; "Defense Suppliers See Laird As Likely Ally for Assault on Cost-Effectiveness System," *Wall Street Journal*, Dec. 12, 1968; "Weapons Costs Put At 50% Over Pentagon Estimates," *Washington Post,* Dec. 30, 1969; "Thailand Fuel Thefts," *Washington Post*, Jan. 1, 1969; "Laird to Weigh Cancellation of Crash-Prone F-111 Plane," *Washington Post*, Jan. 12, 1970; "Dunne Bares U.S. Probe of Medicare Pay," *Chicago Tribune*, May 16, 1969; "Status of GAO Investigations," *Cleveland Press*, May 17, 1969; "Rat Poison Fatal to Tots is Still Sold," *Washington Post*, May 18, 1969; "Auditors for Congress Criticize Head Start Program in County," *Los Angeles Times*, Feb. 19, 1969; "JOBS Plan Criticized by the GAO," *Washington Post*, May 6, 1970; and "Shultz Rebuts Charges Against JOBS Program," *Washington Post,* May 12, 1970.

course of research for this book disclosed that this problem is all too common. When, during the 1960s the GAO attempted again and again to collect and assemble data for the Senate Committee on Government Operations on the controversial TFX airplane, it was denied access to basic information. While it is undoubtedly true that this problem gets one involved in the very hazy constitutional area of executive privilege and the executive's occasional right to withhold certain information, equally important questions arise concerning meaningful legislative oversight and access to vital documents. This dilemma is one which cries out for additional research and an attempt to establish badly needed guidelines. The GAO supplies many facts that otherwise would not reach Congress. No other source, as far as is known, provides this type of analytic information that is so necessary to Congress. As was pointed out in the earlier discussion of the public audit, it is extremely difficult to hold public officials accountable without subjecting these officials to the audit process. Thus, the GAO's seemingly modest task of auditing and reporting on agency activities, programs, and the use of public moneys is, in reality, an indispensable informational aid to Congress and, hence, of great significance to representative government.

I

In sum, it would appear that the GAO performance, when measured against the six criteria just considered, and when viewed in the context of the GAO's present mandate, is a creditable one. Moreover, the performance rating holds up in the face of most of the complaints commonly lodged against the GAO. Some of those not previously mentioned are discussed briefly in the following paragraphs.

One of the most simplistic yet serious criticisms levied at the GAO is typified by a statement in an important book by Keefe and Ogul, *The American Legislative Process,* which says that "the General Accounting Office . . . is concerned mainly with the legality of executive expenditures and not with their utility or wisdom."[13] This frequently heard charge cannot be taken at face value. Indeed, one might argue that an inquiry into the utility and wisdom of governmental expenditures is a main tenet of the GAO's comprehensive audit approach.

Another common charge is that the appropriations committees in Congress do not make use of the GAO or its findings.[14] In view of the research findings that have been presented here, especially with reference to TVA, this criticism cannot be substantiated. Indeed, the findings of Richard Fenno, a distinguished student of Congress, also temper this charge. Although Fenno sees room for improvement, he calls particular attention to the usefulness of the GAO to the Appropriations Committee in the House. Committee Chairman George Mahon himself has commented on the help the committee receives from the GAO.[15]

The GAO has also been criticized for not making greater use of section 206 of the Legislative Reorganization Act of 1946, which authorized the comptroller general to make an expenditure analysis of each agency to help Congress determine whether public funds had been economically and efficiently expended.[16] This criticism, widely noted in current literature, is nullified by the fact that the GAO's increased use of the comprehensive audit device, patterned after the audit techniques set out in the 1945 Corporation Control Act, has made implementation of section 206 unnecessary. Frank Weitzel, then acting comptroller general, clarified this point when he stated before the Joint Committee on the Organization of the Congress:

> The Legislative Reorganization Act of 1946 . . . included section 206 requiring us to make an "expenditure analysis" of each agency in the executive branch. . . . Although Congress declined to appropriate funds for this purpose . . . we believe that the basic objective is being fulfilled to a large extent by our comprehensive audits and the hundreds of reports each year thereon to the Congress concerning economy and efficiency

[13] P. 423.

[14] Clapp, *The Congressman*, p. 219; and Saloma, *The Responsible Use of Power*, p. 81.

[15] Fenno, *The Power of the Purse*, p. 155.

[16] Among others, see Wallace, *Congressional Control*, chs. 11 and 12; Saloma, *The Responsible Use of Power*, pp. 38–39, 81.

in agency operations. However, if the Congress should give us specific guidelines for implementing section 206 and the necessary appropriations, you are assured that we will make every effort to carry out the will of the Congress.[17]

A further argument made by GAO critics is that the GAO serves as a "middleman" between Congress and the executive agencies and, as such, is essentially detrimental to "true" supervision by Congress. To the contrary, congressional supervision is weakened only because Congress has been reluctant to use all the resources and powers of the GAO that the law allows.[18] There is no evidence that Congress's powers of supervision over the executive branch of government are diminished by the fact that the GAO, as an "administrative middleman," does much of the Congress's detailed work. Congressional supervision is a meaningless term unless the machinery exists to provide such supervision. Congressmen rely on their staffs, and the staffs, in turn, rely on whatever the various agencies tell them about their programs. For congressional staffs are already far too busy to carry out the exhaustive research on agency programs that is commonplace to GAO auditors.[19] In short, the GAO is geared to provide the very information that would otherwise not be available to congressmen—the information that alone can give meaning to their supervisory activities. Even though the GAO may sometimes fail in providing it, accurate, detailed, and reliable information on executive operations is one of the great needs of Congress. In this connection, political scientist Ralph Huitt wrote: "The bureaucracy . . . is a matchless device for assembling all kinds of facts, for taking into account all kinds of expert advice. Congress itself is ultimately utterly dependent on the bureaucracy for most of the information upon which it acts." And Senator Abraham Ribicoff, at a committee hearing, indicated that he would agree with this view: "Basically, we are asking whether the GAO can

[17] U.S., Congress, Joint Committee. *Hearings, Organization of the Congress*, 89th Cong., 1st sess., 1965, Pt. 9, p. 1370.

[18] For example, see Wallace, *Congressional Control*, especially chs. 11 and 12.

[19] For discussions on this point, see Clapp, *The Congressman*, especially pp. 263–64; A. D. Little, Inc., *Management Study*, p. 25.

provide the Congress with the kind of information the executive branch is able to provide for itself. Throughout government, the executive branch exercises a virtual monopoly on information regarding federal programs."[20]

Critics of the GAO, and of Congress's use of the GAO, maintain that Congress rarely, if ever, makes a really complete and searching review of an executive agency's operations at any one time. This situation is undoubtedly true, but Congress does not demand it of the GAO and, in fact, congressional organization discourages such an approach. That is why, in recent years, the GAO has been making briefer, more specialized audit reports to Congress. GAO's former documents had been criticized as being too long, detailed, and repetitious for practical and quick use. The new technique, covering a shorter period and being limited to a few very timely or pressing issues, has proved more satisfactory to both the GAO and Congress.

Given the form and procedure of congressional operations, this evolution in the GAO's reporting technique is not surprising. It must be remembered that government operations, appropriations, and legislative committees all work at the business of overseeing governmental programs and performance—separately, in conjunction with each other, and in cooperation with the GAO; thus, conflicts, duplication, and overlapping are inevitable. And, thus, it has come to be more and more accepted that the audit process, like the American budget process, is experimental, fragmented, and incremental; and that auditors, like budgeteers, attempt not to maximize but to "satisfice (satisfy and suffice)." Wildavsky warns:

> In appraising the budgetary process, we must deal with real men in the real world for whom the best they can get is to be preferred to the perfection they cannot achieve. Unwilling or unable to alter the basic features of the political system, they seek to make it work for them in budgeting rather than against them.[21]

[20] Huitt, "Congress, the Durable Partner," in Huitt and Peabody, *Congress: Two Decades of Analysis*, p. 215; "GAO Pondering Audits of Defense Suppliers," *Federal Times*, Oct. 1, 1969.
[21] From *The Politics of the Budgetary Process*, by Aaron Wildavsky,

Read *audit* for *budgetary,* and *auditing* for *budgeting,* and the quotation is equally apt. The GAO, in its audit role, is thus called upon to serve many congressional committees with overlapping mandates and changing and varied interests. Its auditing and reporting techniques must therefore remain flexible, and its audit reports must be manageable in form and content.

The charge of "congressional meddling" in the executive branch, and the GAO's work as a contribution to this meddling, is also widespread. Clinton Rossiter, for example, is concerned over the trend of Congress to try to direct the executive branch:

> The result has been disorder, dissension, indecision, and disruption of morale at key points in the public service . . . . It is the members of Congress, operating as committees, subcommittees, or lone wolves, who have poked their inquiring noses beyond the limits of political decorum and constitutional practice.[22]

Joseph Harris ties this concern more specifically to Congress's use of the GAO.

> The GAO's restrictions often seem to go beyond the reasonable requirements of protecting the public purse, and amount to a substitution of the Comptroller General's judgment for that of the responsible administrators, even on matters about which the administrators are best situated to judge. The result is a serious limitation on administrative discretion, approaching a transgression on the constitutional authority of the Executive branch.[23]

Yet, the research for this book disclosed no serious cases in the more recent history of the GAO that even remotely fit the above description. It has already been shown that, in its early years, the GAO employed methods that were indeed questionable.

American political scientists, as well as a large part of the pub-

---

(Copyright © 1964, by Little, Brown and Company, Inc.). Concepts of experimentation, fragmentation, and incrementalism in the budgeting process are discussed by Wildavsky in this book. For a discussion of "satisficing," see Herbert A. Simon, *Administrative Behavior: A Study of Decision-Making Processes in Administrative Organization* (New York: The Free Press, 1965).

[22] Clinton Rossiter, *The American Presidency* (New York: Harcourt Brace Jovanovich, Inc., 1960), p. 242.

[23] Harris, *Congressional Control,* p. 146.

lic in general, have too long been fascinated with executive power. If this statement seems biased, it may be fairly asserted that it is high time for some weight to be added to the congressional side of the balance. Rossiter urges: " 'Leave Your Presidencey Alone' that is the message . . . ."[24] Agreed—but with this new emphasis: "Let us strengthen Congress, in part through the GAO." Then, whether the constitutional convention of 1787 created a government of "separated powers" or "a government of separated institutions sharing powers,"[25] the nation will have executive and legislative branches of equal power and imaginative scope. Too often the "sharing of powers" by these two governmental branches is regarded as a one-way street, with the executive branch eager to share the traditional powers of Congress but quick to call constitutional foul when it appears the reverse might occur. Bertram M. Gross, in commenting upon the possible tasks of a new Hoover-type commission, recognized this problem: "The Commission should be asked to give special attention to . . . developing a meaningful alternative to the prevailing premise concerning executive agency relations with the Congress: namely, that the Executive can be strong only if the Congress is weak."[26]

Finally, there is a class of complaints and laments which comes from American political scientists who are fascinated by the British governmental system and who refuse to recognize that the American system is, and will remain, different from that of Great Britain. The GAO is quite unlike anything the British use and is, therefore, particularly repugnant to this group of theorists. This attitude persists in spite of the research and writings of Don K. Price and others. For example, Price wrote in 1943:

> Perhaps only a psychoanalyst could explain America's peculiar nostalgia for the obsolescent political institutions of the mother country, but the persistence of her obsession with the

[24] Rossiter, *American Presidency*, p. 249.
[25] Richard E. Neustadt, *Presidential Power: The Politics of Leadership* (New York: The New American Library, 1964), p. 42.
[26] "What, Another Hoover Commission?", Testimony of Bertram M. Gross, James A. Norton, and Harvey Sherman, *Public Administration Review*, XXVIII (Mar.–Apr., 1968), 168.

parliamentary system makes it not only an interesting theoretical problem but a practical political and administrative issue . . . .

In appraising their systems of legislative-executive relations, the British and the Americans are both inclined to make the classic theory of parliamentary government their touchstone. Neither nation can really make it work under twentieth-century conditions, but both are curiously fascinated by it and judge the systems as they actually exist in terms of patterns that are now dead.[27]

E. L. Normanton, in his comparative study *Accountability and Audit of Governments,* reached a similar conclusion:

The time is long past when it was sufficient to conclude that British administrative institutions were the best in the world, merely because they were British. They were designed in and for the classic age of parliamentary finance, and it may be that in the classic period the value judgment was justified.[28]

Furthermore, Arthur D. Little, Inc. consultants Philip Donham and Robert Fahey report that the A. D. Little congressional study team also looked into this question and found "essentially that the Commons is a distinctively British institution not adaptable to American purposes, and that there is no cause for the sense of inferiority so many Americans feel when they compare the Commons and Congress."[29]

America, of course, should not be reluctant to borrow from another government any idea or piece of administrative machinery that will help this country get the job done. On the other

[27] Don K. Price, "The Parliamentary and Presidential Systems," *Public Administration Review,* III (Autumn, 1943), 317, 332.

[28] Praeger Publishers, Inc., and Manchester University Press, Manchester, 1966, pp. 423–24. Used by permission. The concern American political scientists continue to show in British institutions rarely takes into account the efforts of British theorists and practitioners to borrow from American governmental experience. For example, the British are becoming more and more interested in the U.S. Congress's committee system. See Bernard Crick, *The Reform of Parliament* (London: Weidenfeld and Nicolson, 1964); Andrew Hill and Anthony Whichelow, *What's Wrong With Parliament?* (Baltimore: Penguin Books, 1964); and Robert Benewick and Robert E. Dowse, eds., *Readings On British Politics and Government* (London: University of London Press, Ltd., 1968).

[29] Donham and Fahey, *Congress Needs Help,* p. 19.

hand, in so doing it would be almost suicidal to ignore the special characteristics of the American governmental system—the separate and checking, but cooperating, branches of Government; the federal structure; the realities of American state and local political activity and strength, as opposed to a truly national party system; the fleeting party majorities and loyalties that this system encourages; and the whole character of American political give-and-take in a land where there are no uniform standards of wealth and education required for political activity. Our task is to relinquish a penchant for borrowed or ready-made solutions and to concentrate instead on making incremental changes to improve our own special system.

As a matter of fact, these questions concerning the GAO and its role in serving Congress seem to point not as directly to the GAO as to the much larger issue of the executive-legislative process, and to indicate that something is wrong not with the theory of this process but with its practical operation. In Clapp's *The Congressman: His Work As He Sees It,* the nature of the problem has been identified by congressmen:

> The role of the executive in the committee process is necessarily a major one, for it [the executive branch] not only requests funds from the Congress to carry out its work but it provides the legislature with most of the information on which decisions about executive programs are based.

And, again:

> The trend toward the primacy of the executive branch in the drafting of legislation is another matter of concern to some members of Congress who fear the influence of the legislative branch vis-à-vis the executive is declining. Congress may lose whatever initiative it has possessed and become little more than a judge of the proposals of others . . . .

Lastly:

> . . . It is very difficult to get anything past the Appropriations Committees involving an expenditure of money that has not been requested by the executive. Congress is in a poor position to initiate major new programs independently of those recommended by the administration . . . .

A sore point for many congressmen is the dependence of committees in reaching decisions on information provided by the executive. By selecting which information to provide and which to withhold, they assert, the executive may well determine the fate of legislation instead of leaving the decision to congressional judgment.[30]

The extent to which Congress, congressional committees, and individual congressmen are forced to rely on information that has been previously screened and selected by the executive branch is, to put it mildly, astounding. This condition applies not only to information that Congress needs for its supervisory function, but as well to information it needs to perform a whole range of vital functions, including obtaining analyses to check on the success of existing laws as a guide to future legislation; checking on the extent to which laws are administered in accordance with congressional intent; making wise and expeditious appropriations; and assembling the necessary data with which to initiate proposals, at least occasionally, rather than always merely reacting to proposals made by others.

While the GAO is of great assistance, Congress at present has no way of getting all of the detailed, reliable data that it needs for these functions except in predigested form. The objection to this arrangement is not that the executive branch cannot be trusted to provide accurate information, but that each branch has its own constitutional, statutory, and traditional responsibilities; and each branch is expected, continually, to carry out these responsibilities to the fullest extent as it sees them. The GAO provides one of the few channels through which the more objective type of information may flow to Congress.

Thus, one by one, most criticisms of the GAO can be met or at least minimized when viewed with new or more current information in hand. Given the congressional structure in the United States, the GAO's sustained effort to adjust to the realities of the situation and see that its work is used has been quite effective. The GAO's work seems to satisfy most congressmen partly because

[30] Pp. 272–73, 274, 275.

its audit process and reports are accurate, timely, and complete, and partly because the GAO is tactful in handling controversial issues. The GAO, as it now operates, provides the means for still further improving congressional supervision. Further attention to congressional control of executive operations, for which there is always room, awaits congressional initiative and leadership.

In following the issues raised in the audit reports of the GAO, one might conclude that although the GAO seems to make significant gains in the face of tremendous obstacles, there are few really tangible results. But this conclusion emphasizes a tendency to demand a concrete solution for each problem and minimizes Congress's view of the value of the audit function itself and of the mere fact that it has the GAO's resources at its disposal. If Congress chooses to ignore the GAO's advice, at least it has had the benefit of it; if it dabbles with GAO findings only to drop them before any solution is reached, at least it has had the intrinsic benefit of the three-way communication established among any given agency, the GAO, and Congress itself. Agency officials, always very much aware of next year's budget needs, are influenced by this interchange. When Congress does become interested enough in a GAO recommendation to insist on agency compliance, GAO's findings are viewed with an increased respect by the agency and it is likely to act with greater caution in the future. An interesting but unanswerable question is: Without the GAO to aid Congress, what might agencies then do or not do with regard to satisfying congressional intent? The implied answer measures the importance of the GAO. Charles Hyneman supplies an appropriate conclusion to this chapter on the GAO's present role:

> The GAO . . . falls logically in place, for its position in the structure of government is consistent with the service it is expected to perform. Its principal job is to police the administrative departments and agencies in respect to financial matters. We follow the British tradition, which holds that the representative assembly should keep a firm hand on the raising of money for public use and the appropriation of money for public purposes. It follows that Congress should have a high confidence in the agency that studies and reports on the use which

administrative officials and employees make of the money given them.[31]

This enthusiasm, however, must be tempered by remembering that the GAO aids, but does not replace, the basic responsibility of Congress in supervising public policy and administration.

[31] *Bureaucracy in a Democracy,* p. 384.

VII. WHAT OF GAO'S FUTURE?

THE future of the GAO depends, in the last analysis, on how Congress views its own present strength and its future role as compared to other branches of the government. A consensus favoring a stronger Congress could result in a desire to use the GAO more intensively, increasing congressional reliance upon the services presently available, and also more extensively, adding new services beyond the GAO's present mandate.

A brief look at some of the expanded GAO activities that might result from such a consensus is provided in this chapter. The examination may, at the same time, suggest possible improvements or needed changes in the operations of Congress itself.

There are three services that the GAO, properly strengthened, would be uniquely able to provide: staffing, legislative evaluation (or program analysis), and budget information. Three other services could be provided by the GAO, although they do not necessarily require the special training and competence of GAO personnel: administrative services, regulation of lobbying, and an ombudsman's office.

I

Staffing. Congress is already making wide use of GAO employees to supplement its own staff. Since the Eighty-third Congress, the number of GAO employees borrowed annually by congressional committees has more than quadrupled. For example, during fiscal year 1966, 118 employees were assigned to 20 congressional committees and approximately 13,000 man-days of technical assistance were provided for work directly with and under the control of congressional committees. In fiscal year 1967, GAO representatives testified on 18 occasions before congressional committees, 106 staff members were assigned to the staffs of 23 committees or subcommittees, and 530 reports were furnished to committee chairmen on pending bills. During fiscal year 1968, 120 GAO staff members assisted 4 Senate committees, 9 House committees (which included 8 subcommittees), and 2 joint committees.[1]

However, Congress could advantageously make still further use of supplementary personnel from the GAO. There is ample evidence that Congress neither has sufficient personnel within its own ranks, nor has it enlisted outside help to a great enough extent, to assemble and sift properly the material provided by the executive agencies.[2] In his book *House Out of Order,* Congressman Richard Bolling writes:

> Congress as a whole has not provided itself with staffs of experts to serve as consultants in special areas. It has voted billions of dollars to finance research and development in scientific fields, in programs that are administered by the departments of Defense, Health, Education, and Welfare and the National Aeronautics and Space Administration. Yet it relies for information on guidance on agencies of the executive branch, which often have already determined their own policies on major scientific programs.[3]

On the other hand, some political scientists and congressmen are reluctant to see Congress increase the size of its committee staffs to any great extent.[4] Yet, the fact remains that Congress does need additional staff; if properly supervised by Congress, the GAO could provide valuable supplementary staff for advice and assistance.

[1] General Accounting Office, *Annual Report, 1966, 1967,* and *1968,* pp. 4, 3, and 360–61, respectively.

[2] Clapp, *The Congressman,* p. 263; A. D. Little, Inc., *Management Study,* pp. 24–25; Keefe and Ogul, *American Legislative Process,* pp. 172–77.

[3] P. 234.

[4] Kofmehl, *Professional Staffs,* p. 209; and comments by Congressman George Mahon, chairman of the House Appropriations Committee, in Fenno, *The Power of the Purse,* p. 155.

Legislative Evaluation, or Program Analysis. The suggestion was made by Daniel P. Moynihan that an Office of Legislative Evaluation be established in the GAO to review the program evaluations and Program Planning and Budgeting System (PPB) judgments made by executive departments. He said:

> This office would be staffed by professional social scientists. On occasion they would undertake on their own to assess federal programs . . . but in general their task would be to "evaluate the evaluators" and in this way both maintain and improve the quality of the regular ongoing work of the executive departments in this field, and also routinely make these findings available to the Congress.[5]

Moynihan had no illusions about the immediate results of such an office, but believed that "the long-run effect could be immensely useful, if only because Congress would have some clearer idea than now as to what it is doing."[6]

Fremont J. Lyden, in *Public Administration Review,* questioned the value of Moynihan's suggestion because he saw little significant difference between this role suggested for a new office and the role already being played by the Bureau of the Budget in PPB.[7] But Lyden apparently gives little weight to the important fact that the Bureau of the Budget serves the president while the GAO serves Congress, and that Moynihan's suggestion, therefore, would enable the GAO to fill a real need for Congress.

As an alternative to this suggestion, a controllership function could be established in the GAO "to test the validity and consequences of plans, programs, and policies" as suggested by Arthur D. Little, Inc., in its management study of Congress for NBC News. This controllership function is not significantly different from Moynihan's Office of Legislative Evaluation, and either would work to the same purpose of providing more information for Congress.

It is only fair to mention that the Little report concluded that

[5] Daniel P. Moynihan, "A Crisis of Confidence," *The Public Interest,* No. 7 (Spring, 1967), pp. 9–10.

[6] *Ibid.,* p. 9.

[7] Fremont J. Lyden, "An Office of Legislative Evaluation," *Public Administration Review,* XXVII (June, 1967), 191.

the GAO could not succeed in a controllership function because
(1) industrial experience has shown that the two functions,
audit and control, work better if separated; and (2) the head of
the GAO is a presidential appointee and, therefore, the GAO has
divided loyalties.[8] As to the first point, reliance on industrial experience is debatable at best when applied to governmental administration. The second point can be disposed of merely by
stating that at no time during the research for this book was
there found any indication that divided loyalties affected the
GAO's performance. On the contrary, the law governing the GAO;
the fact that the comptroller general is appointed for fifteen years
and is not eligible for reappointment; and GAO's very history, development, and traditions—all these factors emphasize the fact
that the GAO is a truly congressional agency.

Whether designated by Moynihan's or A. D. Little's label,
Wildavsky's policy analysis,[9] or some other name, the new GAO
function would provide Congress with more information, collected by its own agency, on the strengths and weaknesses of existing programs as a means of guiding future congressional action.
That the GAO could perform this service well is indicated by the
fact that the agency is already active in the PPB, cost-effectiveness,
and program-evaluation areas. Congress recently asked the GAO
to evaluate not only the administrative efficiency of the programs
financed by the Office of Economic Opportunity, but also the
extent to which the objectives of those programs were being
achieved. One committee also requested the GAO to broaden its
activity in the area of manpower program evaluation, and various
legislative proposals call for further GAO cost effectiveness and
program-evaluation work in general.[10]

[8] A. D. Little, Inc., *Management Study*, pp. 23–24.

[9] Wildavsky, "Rescuing Policy Analysis from PPBS," in U.S. Congress,
Joint Economic Committee, *The Analysis and Evaluation of Public Ex-
penditures: The PPB System*, 91st Cong., 1st sess., 1969, Joint Committee
Print, Vol. III, 835–52.

[10] U.S., Congress, Joint Economic Committee, *The Planning-Programming-Budgeting System: Progress and Potentials*, 90th Cong., 1st sess.,
1967, Committee Print, pp. 8–9; a letter from the GAO, Mar. 14, 1968;
General Accounting Office, *Review of Economic Opportunity Programs*
(Washington, D.C.: General Accounting Office, 1969), Mar. 18, 1969;

Budget Information. This service would be closely akin to the legislative-evaluation or program-analysis service, but it would have a more direct application to the budget and appropriations processes. Although this fine distinction exists, possibly the two services could be combined into a single GAO unit. A. D. Little's management study of Congress recommended that an analytical budget-information service be established to supplement the GAO; and, of course, extending the GAO to include it would accomplish the same purpose. This service, according to Little, would (1) test in advance the relative effectiveness of alternative courses of action (cost-effectiveness as against operations analyses), and (2) provide Congress with up-to-date budgetary information with which to test how well an agency's performance followed its plan.[11]

Adding weight to the need for budget information service, Congressman Robert McClory (Republican, Illinois), of the House Republican Task Force, in *We Propose: A Modern Congress,* calls for a greater role to be played by the GAO in the congressional budget process.[12] And Congress itself has already proposed legislation that, if passed, could make the GAO a vital part of the congressional budget process through a stepped-up cost-effectiveness and operations-research assignment to the GAO.[13] Without doubt the GAO, properly strengthened, could provide this valuable service to the appropriations, finance and tax, economic policy, and other congressional committees.

---

and Statement of Comptroller General Elmer B. Staats Before the Subcommittee on Executive Reorganization, Senate Committee on Government Operations, from GAO files, Sept. 16, 1969, pp. 18–20.

[11] A. D. Little, Inc., *Management Study,* p. 31.

[12] Robert McClory, "Reforming the Budgetary and Fiscal Machinery of Congress," in Mary McInnis, ed., *We Propose: A Modern Congress,* particularly pp. 122, 129.

[13] U.S., Congress, Senate, Special Committee on Organization of the Congress, *Legislative Reorganization Act of 1967,* 90th Cong., 1st sess., 1967, Rept. 1, especially pp. 22–23. This bill passed the Senate in the 90th Cong., but did not pass the House. It has been reintroduced in both houses of the 91st Cong. as the Legislative Reorganization Act of 1969. The reasons that it did not pass the House in the previous session appear to be because of provisions other than those affecting the GAO.

II

Administrative Services. One of the additional services that could be performed either by the GAO or by some other agency is that of providing vitally needed administrative help in order to give members of Congress more time to devote to policy and political matters. For example, a central agency could provide computer and mail services, office management assistance, and public relations direction, and it could also operate a central personnel office and a clearing house for handling requests from constituents. The GAO already maintains a special audit staff at the Capitol to furnish professional auditing and accounting assistance on congressional financial problems.[14]

Regulation of Lobbying. To ensure the effective functioning of the Legislative Reorganization Act of 1946, which requires the registration of certain categories of lobbyists, a congressional agency, perhaps the GAO, could be charged with maintaining information about lobby registration (the clerk of the House and the secretary of the Senate now perform this duty), analyzing and handling the data relevant to these registrations, and reporting periodically to Congress on lobbyists' activities. This proposal is a part of the pending legislative reorganization bill.[15]

Ombudsman's Office. There has been considerable discussion about the need for an "administrative counsel for the Congress," a "congressional ombudsman," a "citizen's defender," or a "people's watchdog against abuses of power."[16] Such a public servant could protect the people against inefficiency, maladministration, arrogance, and abuse; provide a central information bureau to

---

[14] General Accounting Office, *Annual Report, 1967,* p. 8.

[15] U.S., Congress, Senate, Special Committee on Organization of the Congress, *Legislative Reorganization Act of 1967,* pp. 12, 53–55. See also footnote 13 above.

[16] For a discussion of some of the important literature and proposals in this area, see Charles S. Ascher, "The Grievance Man or Ombudsmania," *Public Administration Review,* XXVII (June, 1967), pp. 174–78; and Roy V. Peel, ed., *The Ombudsman or Citizen's Defender: A Modern Institution* (Philadelphia: The American Academy of Political and Social Science, 1968).

tell citizens of this large country just where to obtain a particular service; and remind both bureaucrats and citizens that the former exist to serve the latter. It is possible that a unit to perform this service could be established in the GAO.

III

These six possible services indicate that there is much more that could be done to assist Congress in several vital areas. The U.S. General Accounting Office (or, more appropriately, the Congressional Auditing Office), would seem to be the proper agency to take over at least some of these more professionally oriented functions by virtue of the fact that it is "on the scene" and staffed largely by accountants, professional people who either have or can quickly acquire a special competence in this type of work. The particular insight gained by CPA's, for instance, is described in a *Forbes* magazine article that deals with CPA firms entering the field of management consulting:

> The big CPA firms constitute a real threat [to the established consulting firms]. For one thing, a company's auditors are a gold mine of information on what is being done well and what badly. For another, the CPA's training in quantitative measure is peculiarly suited to the age of the computer . . . . After all, the auditors already know the company inside and out.[17]

If Congress saw fit to strengthen or enlarge the GAO to encompass the possible new services, it would, in effect, create a "new" GAO; and would need to develop more effective control of, as well as more extensive use of, this more powerful tool. Both the stepped-up control and wider use might be achieved by combining the House and the Senate committees on government operations into a single Joint Committee on Government Operations. The various other congressional committees would, of course, remain free to use the new agency in coordination with the joint committee. In fact, an important task of the joint committee ideally would be to encourage other committees to use the more

[17] "The Business of Management Consulting," *Forbes* (Nov. 15, 1967), p. 41.

powerful agency. The joint committee would also dramatize the importance of congressional supervision of executive operations and help to focus such supervisory activities within Congress. And still further, the joint committee could help to establish the role of the GAO as a true congressional staff adjunct, possibly to the same extent that the Bureau of the Budget—created by the same 1921 legislation—has become established as the strong right arm of the President. The joint committee, since it would be a collective legislative body, could not hope to operate as efficiently as does a single executive. Still, it could serve as an external check on the GAO while internal control would continue to be exercised by the professional competence and personal integrity of the GAO officials.

IV

This is an age in which sound judgment and wise policy-making are inseparably tied to an understanding of a number of complexities: for example, the intricacy of administrative management, the assembly and use of voluminous quantities of data, and the means of making unwieldy organizations move in desired directions. It may be easier for a chief executive than for a legislative body to reach this understanding and act upon it; but Congress will simply have to work much harder to acquire the same degree of efficiency. Much depends on Congress's achievement of this end. It must regain and retain a positive role in the budgetmaking and legislative processes and at the same time increase its effectiveness in administrative supervision. Originally, the President and Congress had separate and distinct responsibilities, and this situation still exists in theory. But in late years, because presidents have been better able to organize their work and assemble the necessary staff, they have been more successful in carrying out their responsibilities and, it could be argued, congressional responsibilities as well.

In an era of fantastic technology, accompanied by an ever-present risk of nuclear war, the relatively smooth-working machinery of the President's office has come to dominate the

105

scene. However, the need for a Congress that is equally strong, vigorous, imaginative, and efficient is demanded by the democratic ideal. If this ideal has a touch of magic in it, that magic is the clash that continually occurs between the branches of government as well as between informed, interested, and sincere groups of individuals. Every step that weakens this magic—every step towards the clear dominance of one faction over another—is a step away from the democratic ideal.

As long as twenty years ago a congressional committee report stated:

> Considering the services offered by the General Accounting Office altogether, the Congress has at hand an instrumentality not only to enforce more effectively its inherent power of the purse but, also, to provide information required for its determination of fiscal policy and formulation of related legislative programs to meet everchanging and expanding needs of the Government. Although . . . the Comptroller General now is called on for assistance with greater frequency than ever before, even more effective use can and should be made by the Congress, and by individual members, of his reports, recommendations, and services. The General Accounting Office is, after all, the agency of the Congress set up for this purpose and should so be utilized by the Congress to the greatest possible extent.[18]

This statement is still an apt expression of the GAO's present value and future potential. The U.S. General Accounting Office should be utilized by the Congress "to the greatest possible extent." In our time, the Congress cannot long afford to be without such assistance.

---

[18] U.S., Congress, House, Committee on Expenditures in the Executive Departments, *The General Accounting Office,* p. 29.

APPENDIXES

APPENDIX A

U. S. General Accounting Office
Organization Chart
(January, 1970)

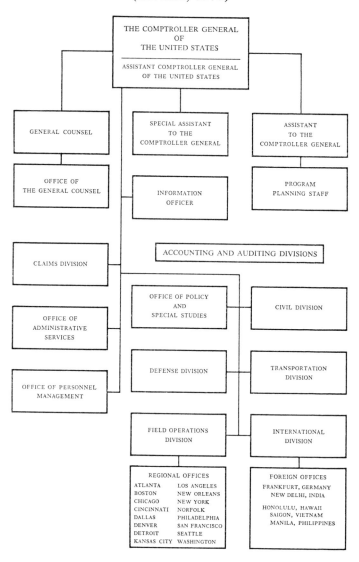

THE COMPTROLLER GENERAL
OF
THE UNITED STATES

ASSISTANT COMPTROLLER GENERAL
OF THE UNITED STATES

GENERAL COUNSEL

SPECIAL ASSISTANT
TO THE
COMPTROLLER GENERAL

ASSISTANT
TO THE
COMPTROLLER GENERAL

OFFICE OF
THE GENERAL COUNSEL

INFORMATION
OFFICER

PROGRAM
PLANNING STAFF

CLAIMS DIVISION

ACCOUNTING AND AUDITING DIVISIONS

OFFICE OF POLICY
AND
SPECIAL STUDIES

CIVIL DIVISION

OFFICE OF
ADMINISTRATIVE
SERVICES

DEFENSE DIVISION

TRANSPORTATION
DIVISION

OFFICE OF PERSONNEL
MANAGEMENT

FIELD OPERATIONS
DIVISION

INTERNATIONAL
DIVISION

REGIONAL OFFICES

ATLANTA	LOS ANGELES
BOSTON	NEW ORLEANS
CHICAGO	NEW YORK
CINCINNATI	NORFOLK
DALLAS	PHILADELPHIA
DENVER	SAN FRANCISCO
DETROIT	SEATTLE
KANSAS CITY	WASHINGTON

FOREIGN OFFICES
FRANKFURT, GERMANY
NEW DELHI, INDIA

HONOLULU, HAWAII
SAIGON, VIETNAM
MANILA, PHILIPPINES

APPENDIX B

LIST OF GAO COMPTROLLERS GENERAL AND ASSISTANT COMPTROLLERS GENERAL

Comptrollers General of the United States

John R. McCarl	July 1, 1921–June 30, 1936
Fred H. Brown	April 11, 1939–June 19, 1940
Lindsay C. Warren	November 1, 1940–April 30, 1954
Joseph Campbell	December 14, 1954–July 31, 1965
Elmer B. Staats	March 8, 1966–

Assistant Comptrollers General of the United States

Lurtin R. Ginn	July 1, 1921–November 11, 1930
Richard N. Elliott	March 9, 1931–April 30, 1943
Frank L. Yates	May 1, 1943–June 29, 1953
Frank H. Weitzel	October 12, 1953–January 17, 1969
Robert F. Keller	October 3, 1969–

BIBLIOGRAPHY

PERSONAL INTERVIEWS[1]

Bailey, Charles M., director, Defense Division, GAO. Aug. 6, 1969.

Calloway, James R., staff director, Senate Committee on Government Operations. Nov. 27, 1968; and other discussions during summer, 1969.

Carlson, John P., minority counsel, House Committee on Government Operations. Jan. 6, 1966.

Cruze, Gifford, comptroller, Tennessee Valley Authority, Knoxville, Tennessee. Feb. 3, 1966.

Eckert, C. E., legislative attorney, Office of Legislative Liaison, Office of the General Counsel, U.S. General Accounting Office. Jan. 4, 1966.

Ellis, L. E., chief, Budget Staff, Office of the General Manager, TVA, Knoxville, Tennessee. Dec. 1, 1965.

Ericson, E. P., assistant to the General Manager (Budget and Planning), TVA, Knoxville, Tennessee. Feb. 3, 1966.

Hall, James T., Jr., assistant director, Civil Accounting and Auditing Division, GAO. Jan. 4, 1966; Feb. 1, 1968.

Hatcher, Kenneth D., assistant to the Comptroller, TVA, Knoxville, Tennessee. Jan. 8, 22, and Feb. 7, 1968.

Indritz, Phineas, chief counsel, Natural Resources and Power Subcommittee, House Committee on Government Operations. Jan. 6, 1966.

Kane, Owen A., legislative attorney, Office of Legislative Liaison, Office of the General Counsel, GAO. Dec. 27, 1967; Feb. 1, 1968; Nov. 27, 1968; and several discussions during summer, 1969.

[1] All interviews were held in Washington, D.C., unless otherwise noted.

Kannerick, Paul E., assistant counsel, Permanent Investigations Subcommittee, Senate Committee on Government Operations. Sept. 18, 1969.

Keller, Robert F., then general counsel, now assistant comptroller general of the United States, GAO. Aug. 19, 1969.

Morse, E. H., Jr., director, Office of Policy and Special Studies, GAO. Feb. 1, 1968; and several discussions during summer, 1969.

Nobleman, Eli E., professional staff member, Senate Committee on Government Operations. Jan. 7, 1966; Dec. 29, 1967.

Owen, Marguerite, Washington representative, TVA. Jan. 4, 1966.

Pearse, Frederic M. P., Jr., attorney, Office of the General Counsel, GAO. Jan. 5, 1966.

Rasco, William, professional staff member, Natural Resources and Power Subcommittee, House Committee on Government Operations. Jan. 6, 1966.

Romney, Miles Q., associate general counsel, House Committee on Government Operations. Jan. 7, 1966.

Shriver, Glen K., professional staff member, Senate Committee on Government Operations. Several discussions during summer, 1969.

Smith, Frederic H., deputy director, Office of Policy and Special Studies, GAO. Several interviews during summer, 1969.

Staats, Elmer B., comptroller general of the United States, GAO. Feb. 1, 1968.

Sullivan, Richard J., chief counsel, House Committee on Public Works. Jan. 6, 1966.

Thompson, L. F., legislative attorney, Office of Legislative Liaison, Office of the General Counsel, GAO. Jan. 5, 1966; several discussions during summer, 1969.

Weitzel, Frank H., assistant comptroller general of the United States, GAO. Feb. 1, 1968; Nov. 27, 1968.

BOOKS

Beer, Samuel H. Treasury Control: *The Coordination of Financial and Economic Policy in Great Britain.* Oxford, England: Clarendon Press, 1956.

Benewick, Robert, and Robert E. Dowse, eds. *Readings on British Politics and Government*. London: University of London Press, Ltd., 1968.

Berman, Daniel M. *In Congress Assembled: The Legislative Process in the National Government*. New York: The Macmillan Company, 1964.

Bolling, Richard. *House Out of Order*. New York: E. P. Dutton and Co., Inc., 1965.

Clapp, Charles L. *The Congressman: His Work As He Sees It*. Washington, D.C.: Brookings Institution, 1963.

Clark, Joseph S. *Congress: The Sapless Branch*. New York: Harper and Row, Publishers, 1964.

Crick, Bernard. *The Reform of Parliament*. London: Weidenfeld and Nicolson, 1964.

DeGrazia, Alfred, ed. *Congress: The First Branch of Government*. Garden City, N. Y.: Anchor Books, Doubleday and Company, Inc., 1967.

Donham, Philip, and Robert J. Fahey. *Congress Needs Help*. New York: Random House, 1966.

Emmerich, Herbert. *Essays On Federal Reorganization*. University, Ala.: University of Alabama Press, 1950.

Fenno, Richard F., Jr. *The Power of the Purse: Appropriations Politics in Congress*. Boston: Little, Brown and Company, 1966.

Fesler, James W. *Area and Administration*. University, Ala.: University of Alabama Press, 1949.

Galbraith, John Kenneth. *American Capitalism: The Concept of Countervailing Power*. Houghton Mifflin Company, 1956.

Galloway, George B. *Congress at the Crossroads*. New York: Thomas Y. Crowell Company, 1946.

————. *The Legislative Process in Congress*. New York: Thomas Y. Crowell Company, 1955.

Gilmour, Ian. *The Body Politic*. London: Hutchinson and Co., Ltd., 1969.

Green, Harold P., and Alan Rosenthal. *Government of the Atom*. New York: Atherton Press, 1964.

Harris, Joseph P. *Congressional Control of Administration.* Washington, D.C.: Brookings Institution, 1964.

Hill, Andrew, and Anthony Whichelow. *What's Wrong With Parliament?* Baltimore: Penguin Books, 1964.

Huitt, Ralph K., and Robert L. Peabody. *Congress: Two Decades of Analysis.* New York: Harper and Row, Publishers, 1969.

Hyneman, Charles S. *Bureaucracy in a Democracy.* New York: Harper and Brothers Publishers, 1950.

Keefe, William J., and Morris S. Ogul. *The American Legislative Process: Congress and the States.* Englewood Cliffs, N. J.: Prentice-Hall, Inc., 1964.

Kofmehl, Kenneth. *Professional Staffs of Congress.* Lafayette, Ind.: Purdue University Studies, 1962.

Lilienthal, David E. *The TVA Years, 1939–1945.* Vol. I of *The Journals of David E. Lilienthal.* New York: Harper and Row, Publishers, 1964.

Little, Arthur D., Inc. *Management Study of the U.S. Congress.* Cambridge, Mass., 1965.

McInnis, Mary, ed. *We Propose: A Modern Congress.* New York: McGraw-Hill Book Company, 1966.

Mansfield, Harvey C. *The Comptroller General: A Study in the Law and Practice of Financial Administration.* New Haven: Yale University Press, 1939.

Marx, Fritz Morstein, ed. *Elements of Public Administration.* Englewood Cliffs, N. J.: Prentice-Hall, Inc., 1959.

Millett, John D. *Government and Public Administration: The Quest for Responsible Performance.* New York: McGraw-Hill Book Company, Inc., 1959.

Neustadt, Richard E. *Presidential Power: The Politics of Leadership.* New York: The New American Library, 1964.

Normanton, E. L. *Accountability and Audit of Governments: A Comparative Study.* New York: Praeger Publishers, Inc., and Manchester University Press, Manchester, 1966.

Peabody, Robert L., and Nelson W. Polsby. *New Perspectives on the House of Representatives.* Chicago: Rand McNally and Co., 1963.

Peel, Roy V., ed. *The Ombudsman Or Citizen's Defender: A Modern Institution.* Philadelphia: The American Academy of Political and Social Science, 1968.

Pritchett, C. Herman. *The Tennessee Valley Authority: A Study in Public Administration.* Chapel Hill: The University of North Carolina Press, 1943.

Ranney, Austin, ed. *Political Science and Public Policy.* Chicago: Markham Publishing Company, 1968.

Rossiter, Clinton. *The American Presidency.* New York: Harcourt Brace Jovanovich, Inc., 1960.

Saloma, John S. II. *The Responsible Use of Power: A Critical Analysis of the Congressional Budget Process.* Washington, D.C.: American Enterprise Institute for Public Policy Research, 1964.

Schulsinger, Gerald G. *The General Accounting Office: Two Glimpses:* Case No. 35, Inter-University Case Program Series. University, Ala.: University of Alabama Press, 1956.

Simon, Herbert A. *Administrative Behavior: A Study of Decision-Making Processes in Administrative Organization.* New York: The Free Press, 1965.

Smithies, Arthur. *The Budgetary Process in the United States.* New York, Toronto, and London: McGraw-Hill Book Company, Inc., 1955.

Truman, David B., ed. *The Congress and America's Future.* Englewood Cliffs, N. J.: Prentice-Hall, Inc., 1965.

Wallace, Robert A. *Congressional Control of Federal Spending.* Detroit: Wayne State University Press, 1960.

Wildavsky, Aaron. *Dixon-Yates: A Study in Power Politics.* New Haven and London: Yale University Press, 1962.

———. *The Politics of the Budgetary Process.* Boston and Toronto: Little, Brown and Company, 1964.

Wiseman, H. V. *Parliament and the Executive.* London: Routledge and Kegan Paul, Ltd., 1966.

PUBLIC DOCUMENTS

Congressional Hearings and Reports

U.S. Congress. Joint Committee. *Hearings, Investigation of the*

Tennessee Valley Authority. 75th Cong., 3rd sess., 1938, Pts. 13 and 14.

————. Joint Committee. *Hearings, Organization of the Congress.* 89th Cong., 1st sess., 1965, Pt. 9.

————. Joint Committee. *Report on the Investigation of the Tennessee Valley Authority.* 76th Cong., 1st sess., 1939, Senate Doc. No. 56.

————. Joint Economic Committee. *Hearings, Impact of Military and Related Civilian Supply and Service Activities on the Economy.* 88th Cong., 1st and 2nd sess., 1963, 1964.

————. Joint Economic Committee. *Hearings, Interest Rate Guidelines For Federal Decision-making.* 90th Cong., 2nd sess., 1968.

————. Joint Economic Committee. *Report on the Planning-Programming-Budgeting System: Progress and Potentials.* 90th Cong., 1st sess., 1967, Committee Print.

————. Joint Economic Committee. *The Analysis and Evaluation of Public Expenditures: The PPB System.* 91st Cong., 1st sess., 1969, Committee Print, Vol. III.

————. House and Senate committees on government operations. *Joint Hearings, Five Year Record of the Advisory Commission on Intergovernmental Relations and Its Future Role.* 89th Cong., 1st sess., 1965.

U.S. House of Representatives. Committee on Appropriations. *Hearings on the Department of Defense Appropriations (1962).* 87th Cong., 1st sess., 1961.

————. Committee on Appropriations. *Hearings on the General Accounting Office, Independent Offices (1957–1964 and 1966–67).* 85th–90th Congs.

————. Committee on Appropriations. *Hearings on the General Accounting Office, Legislative Branch Appropriations (1965 and 1968–70).* 89th–91st Cong.

————. Committee on Appropriations. *Hearings on Tennessee Valley Authority, Public Works (1957–1966).* 85th–89th Congs.

————. Committee on Expenditures in the Executive Departments. *The General Accounting Office: A Study of Its Func-*

tions and Operations. 81st Cong., 1st sess., 1949, Rept. 1441.

————. Committee on Government Operations. *Activities of the House Committee on Government Operations.* 85th–89th Congs. Issued during the 1st sess. of the 86th–90th Congs., in 1959, 1961, 1963, 1965, and 1967, respectively.

————. Committee on Government Operations. *Composition, Jurisdiction, and Authority of the Natural Resources and Power Subcommittee of the Committee on Government Operations.* 89th Cong., 1st sess., 1965, mimeographed piece.

————. Committee on Government Operations. *Extent of the Control of the Executive by the Congress of the United States.* 87th Cong., 2nd sess., 1962, Committee Print, by Charles J. Zinn.

————. Committee on Government Operations. *The General Accounting Office: A Study of Its Organization and Administration with Recommendations for Increasing Effectiveness.* 84th Cong., 2nd sess., 1956, Rept. 2264.

————. Committee on Government Operations. *Hearings, Tennessee Valley Authority Urgent Purchases.* 87th Cong., 2nd sess., 1962, Rept. 2152.

————. Committee on Government Operations. *Interim Report for the House Committee.* 90th Cong., 2nd sess., Feb. 5, 1968.

————. Committee on Government Operations. *Legislative Calendar.* 90th Cong., 1st sess., Dec. 28, 1967.

————. Committee on Government Operations. *Notes on the Jurisdiction of the House Committee on Government Operations.* 86th Cong., 1st sess., 1959.

————. Committee on Government Operations. *Tennessee Valley Authority Urgent Purchases.* 87th Cong., 2nd sess., 1962, Rept. 2152.

————. Committee on Public Works. *Hearings, Real Property Acquisition Practices.* 88th Cong., 1st sess., 1963.

————. Committee on Public Works. *Hearings, Tennessee Valley Authority.* 86th Cong., 1st sess., 1959.

————. Committee on Public Works. *Hearings, Tennessee Valley Authority Financing.* 85th Cong., 1st sess., 1957.

————. Committee on Public Works. *Study of Compensation*

and Assistance for Persons Affected by Real Property Acquisition in Federal and Federally Assisted Programs. 88th Cong., 2nd sess., 1964, Committee Print No. 31.

——. Committee on Public Works. *TVA-Trial by Jury.* 90th Cong., 2nd sess., 1968, Rept. 1840.

U.S. Senate. Committee on Appropriations. *Hearings on the General Accounting Office, Independent Offices (1957–1964 and 1966–1967).* 85th–90th Congs.

——. Committee on Appropriations. *Hearings on the General Accounting Office, Legislative Branch Appropriations (1965 and 1968–70).* 89th–91st Congs.

——. Committee on Appropriations. *Hearings on Tennessee Valley Authority, Public Works (1957–1966).* 85th–89th Congs.

——. Committee on Government Operations. *Activities Reports of the Senate Committee on Government Operations.* 85th–89th Congs. Issued during the 1st sess. of the 86th–90th Congs., in 1959, 1961, 1963, 1965, and 1967, respectively.

——. Committee on Government Operations. *Financial Management in the Federal Government.* 87th Cong., 1st sess., 1961, Doc. No. 11, Pt. 1.

——. Committee on Government Operations. *Functions of the General Accounting Office.* 87th Cong., 2nd sess., 1962, Doc. No. 96.

——. Committee on Government Operations. *Legislative Calendar.* 90th Cong., 1st sess., Nov. 4, 1967.

——. Committee on Government Operations. *Review of Audit Reports of the Comptroller General.* 84th Cong., 2nd sess., 1956, Rept. 1572.

——. Committee on Public Works. *Hearings, Amending the Tennessee Valley Act.* 85th Cong., 1st sess., 1957.

——. Committee on Public Works. *Revenue Bond Financing by TVA.* 86th Cong., 1st sess., 1959.

——. Special Committee on the Organization of the Congress. *Legislative Reorganization Act of 1967.* 90th Cong., 1st sess., 1967, Rept. 1.

Other Public Documents

U.S. Commission on Organization of the Executive Branch of the Government (New Hoover Commission). *Digests and Analyses of the Nineteen Hoover Commission Reports.* Washington, D.C.: Citizens Committee for the Hoover Report, 1955.

———. (First Hoover Commission). *The Hoover Commission Report.* New York: McGraw-Hill Book Company, Inc., 1949.

U.S. General Accounting Office. *Annual Reports of the Comptroller General of the United States (Fiscal years 1952 and 1957–1969).* Washington, D.C.: U.S. Government Printing Office, published annually.

———. *Audit Reports to the Congress of the United States on the Activities of the Tennessee Valley Authority (Fiscal Years 1945 and 1957–1968).* Washington, D.C.: General Accounting Office.

———. *The Joint Financial Management Improvement Program: Annual Reports for Fiscal Years 1961–1968.* Washington, D.C.: U. S. Government Printing Office.

———. Materials, including newspaper accounts, from the files.

———. *Report on Review of Fertilizer, Agricultural, and Munitions Program of the Tennessee Valley Authority, Fiscal Year 1958.* Washington, D.C.: General Accounting Office, 1959.

———. *Report to the Congress: Sale of Hydroelectric Power by the Department of Interior Under Section 5 of the Flood Control Act of 1944 at Rates Not Approved by the Federal Power Commission.* Washington, D.C.: General Accounting Office, 1964.

———. *Review of Economic Opportunity Programs.* Washington, D.C.: General Accounting Office, 1969.

———. *Short Form Report on Audit of Tennessee Valley Authority, Fiscal Year 1959.* Washington, D.C.: General Accounting Office, 1959.

———. *15 Years of Progress: Improvement of Financial Management in the United States Government.* Washington, D.C.: U.S. Government Printing Office, 1963.

U.S. President's Committee on Administrative Management. *Administrative Management in the Government of the United States*. Washington, D.C.: U.S. Government Printing Office, 1937.

U.S. Tennessee Valley Authority. *Budget Program for Fiscal Year 1970*. Knoxville, 1968.

———. *Financial Statements for Fiscal Year 1966*. (Audit by Lybrand, Ross Bros., and Montgomery). Knoxville, 1966.

———. General manager's files, including newspaper accounts.

———. *Handbook*. Knoxville.

———. *Land Acquisition in TVA*. (Statements Presented Before the Select Subcommittee on Real Property Acquisition of the House Committee on Public Works.) Chattanooga: TVA, Division of Property and Supply, 1963.

———. *The Division of Finance of the Tennessee Valley Authority*. Knoxville, 1958.

U.S., *42 Statutes at Large* 20 (1921) and *59 Statutes at Large* 616 (1945).

ARTICLES

Ascher, Charles S. "The Grievance Man or Ombudsmania," *Public Administration Review*, XXVII (June, 1967), 174–78.

"The Business of Management Consulting," *Forbes*, C (Nov. 15, 1967), 27–41.

Kennan, George F. "America's Administrative Response to Its World Problems," *Daedalus*, LXXXVII (Spring, 1958), 5–24.

Lyden, Fremont J. "An Office of Legislative Evaluation?," *Public Administration Review*, XXVII (June, 1967), 191.

McCall, Andrew F., and Zane Geier. "A Teamwork Venture with Public Accountants in the Audit of TVA," *GAO Review* (Winter, 1968).

McClory, Robert. "Reforming the Budgetary and Fiscal Machinery of Congress," in Mary McInnis, ed., *We Propose: A Modern Congress*, particularly pp. 122, 129.

Methvin, Eugene H. "Is Congress Destroying Itself?," *The Reader's Digest* (Apr., 1969), pp. 65–70.

Moynihan, Daniel P. "A Crisis of Confidence," *The Public Interest,* No. 7 (Spring, 1967), pp. 3–10.

Polsby, Nelson W. "Policy Analysis and Congress," in U.S., Congress, Joint Economic Committee, *The Analysis and Evaluation of Public Expenditures: The PPB System,* 91st Cong., 1st sess., 1969, Joint Committee Print, Vol. III, 944–47.

Price, Don K. "The Parliamentary and Presidential Systems," *Public Administration Review,* III (Autumn, 1943), 317–34.

Staats, Elmer B. "The GAO: Present and Future," *Public Administration Review,* XXVIII (Sept.–Oct., 1968), 461–65.

Steinberg, Alfred. "GAO: The Taxpayer's Best Friend," Reprint from *The Reader's Digest* (Nov., 1967 issue).

"What, Another Hoover Commission?," Testimony by Bertram M. Gross, James A. Norton, and Harvey Sherman, *Public Administration Review,* XXVIII (Mar.–Apr., 1968), 168–80.

Wildavsky, Aaron. "Rescuing Policy Analysis from PPBS," Joint Economic Committee, *The Analysis and Evaluation of Public Expenditures: The PPB System,* 91st Cong., 1st sess., 1969, Committee Print, Vol. III, 835–52.

CORRESPONDENCE

Kane, Owen A., legislative attorney, Office of Legislative Liaison, Office of the General Counsel, GAO. Feb. 2, 1968.

Lanigan, James A., general counsel, Committee on Government Operations, House of Representatives. Feb. 5, 1968.

Morse, E. H., Jr., director, Office of Policy and Special Studies, GAO. Jan. 24, Feb. 5, and Mar. 14, 1968.

Powers, Lawrence J., assistant to the Comptroller General, GAO. Feb. 1, 1968.

Smith, Frederic H., deputy director, Office of Policy and Special Studies, GAO. Jan. 7, 1970.

INDEX

124

post-audit and pre-audit, 73–74
recommendations not always followed by Congress, 33–34, 46–49, 59, 81
reports to the Congress and use made of them, 17–18, 26–27, 28–31, 40–44, 46, 49–52, 64–66, 75, 76–80; *see also Annual Report of the Comptroller General*
scope and duties, 5–7, 17
staff, 16–17, 69–70, 80–81, 98–99
standards for, 72–87
and TVA, *see* Tennessee Valley Authority
Government Corporation Control Act of 1945, 11–12, 13, 21, 23, 24, 26, 36, 37, 59, 60, 73, 74, 88
Government corporations, 11–12, 13, 18–19, 22–24, 60, 74
Gross, Bertram M., *quoted,* 92

H

Harris, Joseph, 72; *quoted,* 46–47, 70–71, 76, 91
Hill, Lister, 47–48, 49
Hoover Commission on Organization of the Executive Branch of the Government, 14–15
Huitt, Ralph, *quoted,* 89
Hyneman, Charles, *quoted,* 14, 61, 96–97

I

Internal administrative checks on funds, 10–11
Interest-rate policy, 79

J

Jensen, Ben F., 50, 51
Joint accounting improvement program, 12, 13, 15, 74n
Joint Committee on Government Operations (proposed), 104–105
Joint Committee on the Organization of Congress, 88

Joint Committee (on the TVA), 21–22
Joint Economic Committee, 79
Jonas, Charles R., 69
Jones, Robert E., 48

K

Keefe, William J., *quoted,* 87–88
Kerr, Robert, 49
Kofmehl, Kenneth, *quoted,* 65
Kohler, E. L., *quoted,* 20–21

L

Law, and the GAO, *see* specific acts, *e.g.,* Budget and Accounting Act of 1921
Legislative Reorganization Act, 1946, 12, 26–27, 41–42, 88–89, 103
Legislative Reorganization Act of 1967 (proposed), 102n
Lilienthal, David, *quoted,* 57–58
Lobbying, 103
Lockheed Aircraft Corporation, 85
Lybrand, Ross Bros., and Montgomery (accounting firm), 36
Lyden, Fremont J., 100

M

McCarl, John R., 18–19
McClory, Robert, 102
McKellar, Kenneth D., 57–58
McNamara, Robert, 61n, 83; *quoted,* 84, 85–86
Madden, Martin B., *quoted,* 64
Magnuson, Warren G., *quoted,* 68–69
Mahon, George, 83, 88
Mansfield, Harvey, *cited,* 5, 18; *quoted,* 58–59
Melton Hill Dam and Reservoir, 29–30
Military Affairs Committee (House), 20
Military-fuel scandal in Thailand, 85
Millett, John, *quoted,* 15–16

125

THE GAO has been cast on the Linotype in ten point Times Roman with two-point spacing between the lines. Handset Times Roman was selected for display. The book was designed by Jim Billingsley, composed and printed by Heritage Printers, Inc., Charlotte, North Carolina, and bound by the Becktold Company, St. Louis, Missouri. The paper on which the book is printed is designed for an effective life of at least three hundred years.

THE UNIVERSITY OF TENNESSEE PRESS